Bake your cake
& eat it Too!

D0641768

R&R PUBLICATIONS MARKETING PTY LTD

TAMARA MILSTEIN

Author's Acknowledgments

Special thanks to Katrina Wilson and my wonderfully supportive team at Tamara's Kitchen, who are always available to test or taste another recipe, teach another class, wash another pot etc. etc..

Thank you Brittany, Jordana, Ryan, Corey and Reagan for allowing me to be a successful working mother.

To my students who happily assisted with the testing of these recipes, namely Stephen Frost, Janet O'Connor, Anna Tallacko, Kristine Abrahams, Olivia Eskander, Marg Boffa, Fiona Tuck, Marina Hawthorne, Eleanore Casey, Lyn Dubowitz, Jenny Langley, Chris Burns, Diana Zalewski, Rowena Vonmoger, Pamela Collins, Lynlea Brumley, Cathy Smith, Ann Campbell, Carolyn Smyth and Marian Joseph.

Major credits
Published by:
R&R Publishing Marketing Pty Ltd
(ACN 78 348 105 138)
PO Box 254
Carlton North Victoria 3054
National Toll Free: 1 800 063 296
E-mail: info@randrpublications.com.au
Web: www.randrpublications.com.au
© Richard Carroll
Publisher: Richard Carroll
Author: Tamara Milstein
Food Photography: Andrew Elton
Photographic Assistant: Bill Holdsworth
Food Stylist: Stephane Souvlis
Assistant Home Economist: Jenny Fanshaw
Creative Director: Aisling Gallagher
Cover Designer: Elain Wei Voon Loh
Proofreader: Sarah Russell

The National Library of Australia
Cataloguing-in-Publication Data

Milstein, Tamara, 1965-.
Bake Your Cake and Eat it Too
Bibliography
Includes index.
ISBN: 1-74022-536-8
EAN: 9 781740 225366
1. Cake. 2. Baking 1. Title
641.8653

All rights reserved. No part of this book may be stored, reproduced or transmitted in any form or by any means without written permission of the publisher, except in the case of brief quotations embodied in critical articles and reviews.

First Edition Printed October 1997
Reprinted August 1998, May 2004
This edition printed in December 2005
Computer typeset in Humanst and American Typewriter by:
R&R Publishing Marketing Pty Ltd, Carlton North, VIC, Australia
Printed in China by Max Production Printing Ltd.

The Publishers would like to acknowledge and thank the following contributors for their support and assistance with the provision of materials for photography and food for photography and recipe development:

Villeroy & Boch, Brookvale, NSW, Australia
Accoutrement, Mosman and Woollahra, NSW, Australia
Baytree Kitchen Shop, Woollarah, NSW, Australia
Olson & Blake, Australia

ontents

Introduction

Cakes, tortes, gateaux…no matter where you are in the world, regardless of the country or culture, you'll find one consistent theme – cakes.

Tt is the universal food that binds families together. It is what mother bakes while children are at school. It is the food of choice when celebrating a birthday, anniversary or any other celebration. A cake baked with love is often given to help soften sadness. Indeed, a slice of cake with a cup of tea or coffee helps raise the spirits. Cakes can be fun, cakes can be interesting, but above all, cakes are nurturing. Even a small slice can evoke feelings of love and support, as if your mother or grandmother was there, watching over you.

This cook book is not a compilation of complicated, time consuming recipes from around the world. It is an expression of what real cakes are all about. These are the cakes that your grandmother used to make or that your grandmother's mother used to make. All recipes are easy to follow and do not require any previous baking experience.

Superb photographs will have you dreaming of exotic cakes with fascinating flavour combinations. Imagine serving a Sicilian Apple Cake or Syrian Nut Cake for afternoon tea. How about ending your Indian meal with a slice of Indian Yoghurt Banana Cake or stunning Orange Cardamom Cakes? The Chinese Ginger Syrup Cake will finish any Asian meal superbly, or imagine curling up in front of a log fire with a slice of decadent Mexican Chocolate Cake.

A selection of innovative savoury cakes is also included to make your next buffet or picnic a sure-fire success.

Thumb through the superb recipes within and treat the children, treat your friends, treat yourself – Bake your cake and eat it too!

foreword

Most cake books frighten off novice bakers because the book begins with pages and pages of do's and don'ts. Although these are no doubt helpful, they serve no purpose if the cook decides to close the book in apprehension and drive down to the local bakery to purchase a cake instead of creating one.

This book is different. Each cake recipe is complete, with clear and concise instructions that require no prior knowledge of baking, or cooking for that matter. There is no need to flip to other pages for reference or explanation of cooking terms, and you need concentrate only on the page at hand.

Most of these cakes follow the same simple method: mix some ingredients, combine others, combine both mixtures, pour into a tin, then bake. Perhaps a simple syrup or garnish will complete the recipe, enabling you to bake with success every time.

Remember that these recipes are written with Australian metric measurements in mind, so if you are unsure of your measuring equipment, purchase an Australian measuring jug and measuring spoons, and, as always, use quality scales for measuring such ingredients as flour, where necessary.

The recipes in this chapter are written and tested for fan-forced ovens, so if you are using a gas or electric oven that is not fan-forced, you may need up to 10 minutes longer (baking time) or you may be able to raise the oven heat by 10°C and cook for the time required in the recipe.

Most of all, remember that these cakes are honest, easy interpretations of the flavours of the world. Women in Greece, Italy, Poland or Sri Lanka bake successfully without the most up-to-date equipment, and so can you!

I hope you have as much pleasure baking from this book as I did when I created the book for you.

Bake them, share them, indulge in them!

Happy baking,

Tamara Milstein

The Basics

You've probably noticed that most cake books have a first chapter dedicated to lengthy explanations of various cooking and baking terms, in order to guarantee sure-fire success! The only problem is that by the time you have crawled through the technical information, the desire to bake a cake has vanished.

I want you to enjoy baking the way our mothers and grandmothers did. Each recipe in this book has all the information you need right at your fingertips. This cookbook makes baking a cake easy and fun…the way it should be!

Equipment:

You don't need expensive equipment. A selection of mixing bowls, wooden spoons and whisks should suffice for the preparation of the batter, although, if you have an electric mixer, you may find it useful. If you already have some cake tins, use what you have – there will be plenty of time to purchase new equipment later.

If you are in the market for new cake tins, choose good quality springform tins. Non-stick tins will give you years of service if you treat them carefully and never cut or scrape them with metal objects. Wash them by hand; never put them in the dishwasher.

Preparing your cake tins correctly is crucial. If a recipe calls for buttering or oiling a cake tin, do so thoroughly making sure that the entire surface has been buttered. I find that a light dusting of plain flour over the buttered surface guarantees an easy release of the cake after baking. (If a recipe calls for coating the buttered surface with ground nuts, biscuit crumbs or coconut, omit the light dusting of flour.)

I have finally discovered a surefire way of getting cakes out of the base of a springform tin quickly and easily. Simply remove the sides from the base of the springform tin and place a large piece of baking paper over the base. Replace the side and close the hinge, creating a tight false bottom on the base of the tin. Once the cake has baked and the sides of the tin can be removed, place the cake on a platter and slide the cake tin base out.

Next, ease the paper out from under the cake and voilà…no need to serve the cake still nestled in the metal springform case.

Quality scales and measuring cups are a necessity. Make sure you choose Australian made measuring cups where the metric cup measures 250mL. The small nested sets of plastic measuring cups are also useful, as are tablespoon and teaspoon measures. For absolute ease of measuring, investigate the new scales that can measure liquid, as well as dry ingredients, in imperial and metric measurements.

You will want to make sure that your oven heats accurately. To check, purchase an inexpensive oven thermometer and heat your oven to 200°C. Place the oven thermometer inside and leave it for 30 minutes. Remove the thermometer and check that it registers within 5°C. If not, call a serviceman to re-adjust the oven temperature.

Where a recipe calls for toasted nuts or coconut, try doing this in the microwave oven. Spread the nuts onto the glass microwave plate evenly, then cook on "high" for 2 minutes. Mix a little, then cook on "high" additionally, 1 minute at a time, until the nuts or coconut are as golden as you like.

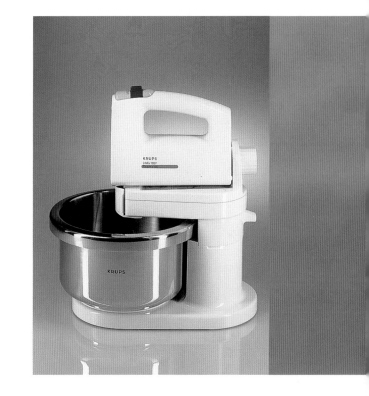

Ingredients:

Quality ingredients are always important. Make sure that your flour is fresh and well aerated. If using wholemeal or rye flour, it is imperative that it is fresh and not rancid. To check, stir a spoonful or two into a glass of warm water. The aroma should be pleasantly floury, not bitter or sour.

Purchase good quality cocoa and chocolate, and store nuts in the freezer so they remain fresher longer. Buy coconut as necessary and make sure that creams, buttermilk and all dairy products are fresh. When using fresh fruit in recipes, ensure they are firm or soft, as the recipe dictates. Using a firm banana where a soft one is called for will change the essence of the recipe.

The **Cakes** *of the* Mediterranean

I love the Mediterranean. Any recipe can take me to a sun-drenched terrace where I imagine sipping a warm caffè latte or light red wine, and letting the hours slip away.

While creating these recipes, I recalled trips to Greece and Italy and imagined trips to Turkey. I have used the classic traditions in these regions to create recipes that will delight you and your guests.

In true Mediterranean style, some of these cakes are soaked in a sweet syrup, designed to enrich the cake and keep it fresh for days.

There are cakes here that will appeal to all tastes – fruit, nuts, spices, citrus, chocolate and herbs all feature, making this a chapter you will want to return to again and again.

Greek Walnut Syrup *Cake*

Many countries dotted around the Mediterranean are famous for sweet, syrupy cakes and desserts, and this one stands out as my favourite. Although the syrup produces a cake that is quite moist and full of sweetness, the walnuts tend to reduce the potency and balance the flavours. It is traditionally served with Greek yoghurt which I like to flavour with citrus. Traditionally, this cake would be baked in a square tin but I prefer to bake it in a round, springform tin to make serving easier.

Ingredients

For the Cake:
130g soft butter
60g sugar
40g brown sugar
8 large eggs, separated
zest of 2 lemons
60g plain flour
2 heaped teaspoons baking powder
1/4 teaspoon salt
1 teaspoon cinnamon
1 teaspoon nutmeg
1/2 teaspoon ground cloves
400g ground walnuts, toasted

For the Syrup:
1 cup of sugar
300mL water
125mL honey
juice and zest of 2 lemons
1 cinnamon stick

Method

1 Generously butter a non-stick 24cm springform tin and set aside. Preheat the oven to 190°C.

2 Beat the soft butter and sugars together until light and fluffy. With the motor running, add the egg yolks one at a time and beat well to incorporate each before adding the next egg yolk. When they have all been incorporated, stir through the zest of the lemons and set aside.

3 In a separate bowl, mix together the plain flour, baking powder, salt, cinnamon, nutmeg and ground cloves. Add this flour mixture to the butter mixture, then add the ground nuts and fold through, taking care to incorporate all the ingredients thoroughly.

4 Meanwhile, beat the egg whites until stiff peaks form, then fold a small amount of the whites into the cake batter. Fold in the remainder of the whites gently.

5 Spoon the cake batter into the prepared tin and bake for 45–55 minutes, or until cooked through.

6 While the cake is baking, prepare the syrup by mixing all the ingredients together and simmer for 10 minutes. Strain to remove solids and set aside.

7 Remove the cake from the oven and pour the hot syrup over the cake. Leave the cake undisturbed until the syrup has been thoroughly absorbed. If this seems to take quite a long time, make some fine holes in the surface of the cake with a toothpick or wooden skewer.

8 To serve, cut into thin slices and accompany with a little Greek yoghurt that has been mixed with some orange, lemon or lime zest.

Turkish Apricot Orange *Cake* (photographed on page 9)

Cakes from countries like Turkey are usually quite sweet and course-textured, designed to be eaten alongside a strong Turkish coffee. The orange flavour is further intensified by an orange and honey syrup poured over the cake after baking. One of the most important ingredients is 'yoghurt cheese' which is made by draining yoghurt of its liquid. In Turkey, you can buy this over the counter, but since it is hard to buy in Australia, I have included a simple method for making it at home. I like to serve this cake with some cinnamon-spiked yoghurt.

Ingredients

500g Greek style plain yoghurt

3 tablespoons pistachio kernels, ground

125g soft butter

¾ cup sugar

zest and juice of 2 oranges

2 large eggs

2 cups self raising flour

1 teaspoon baking powder

1 cup dried Turkish apricots, chopped

1 cup pistachio kernels, chopped

½ cup slivered almonds, toasted

125mL honey

zest of 2 oranges

200mL orange juice

50mL water

10 mint leaves, torn

Method

1 Day before baking: Line a large sieve with muslin and spoon the yoghurt into the sieve. Place this over a bowl and cover with plastic wrap. Allow this to sit undisturbed in the refrigerator for 12 hours. Discard the liquid and set aside the yoghurt.

2 Day of baking: Preheat the oven to 180°C. Generously butter a 28cm or 26cm springform cake tin and sprinkle the ground pistachio nuts around the tin. Tip the tin to help the nuts adhere to the buttered sides.

3 Beat the butter, sugar and orange zest together until thick and pale, then add the eggs one at a time and beat well after each addition. Add the yoghurt and orange juice and continue to beat on a slow speed until the batter is well mixed.

4 In a separate bowl, mix together the flour and baking powder, then sift this into the cake batter. Mix gently but thoroughly and finally add the chopped apricots and nuts, and mix to distribute.

5 Pour the cake batter into the prepared tin and bake for 50 minutes or until 'springy' when pressed gently in the centre.

6 Meanwhile, simmer together the honey, orange zest, orange juice, water and torn mint leaves for 6 minutes.
Strain and set aside.

7 When the cake has finished baking, remove it from the oven and place on a tray or piece of foil to catch any drips. Pour the orange syrup over the cake and allow to cool.

8 Serve with a little yoghurt that has been flavoured with some honey and cinnamon to taste, and orange segments if desired.

Torta *di* Cioccolata
Italian-style Chocolate Cake

This rich, moist chocolate cake will satisfy even the most discriminating chocolate lover. This cake also keeps remarkably well for several days, and I like to serve it warm with ice-cream when it is a few days old. When freshly baked, the cake will have a delicious crisp top that will soften over the next few days.

Ingredients

100g butter

350g good quality chocolate

1 tablespoon instant coffee powder

3 tablespoons Dutch cocoa

5 large eggs

250g caster sugar

5 tablespoons ground walnuts (walnut meal)

100g walnut pieces

1 tablespoon cocoa

1 tablespoon icing sugar

Method

1 Preheat the oven to 180°C and butter a 20cm non-stick springform tin.

2 Place the butter and chocolate, broken into pieces, into a heatproof bowl and set over a saucepan of simmering water (or melt in a microwave). Stir gently until the chocolate is thoroughly melted and the mixture is smooth. Whisk in the coffee powder and cocoa then set aside.

3 In a separate bowl, beat the eggs and sugar together until thick and pale, about 5 minutes, then fold in the walnut meal and walnut pieces.

4 Gently fold together the chocolate mixture and the egg mixture until thoroughly combined, then pour the batter into the prepared cake tin.

5 Bake at 180°C for 40 minutes or until the top of the cake is dry. Turn off the oven and leave the cake undisturbed to cool.

6 When the cake is cool, remove from the cold oven and gently remove from the tin.

7 Dust with a combination of the cocoa and icing sugar and serve in thin slices.

Greek Coconut *and* Fig Cake

This recipe was created in my dreams, after a close friend spent some time travelling the Greek Islands. She described a cake she had eaten in a little cafe in Mikonos, while watching small boats bobbing on the water and working on her suntan. The only detail I could glean was that the cake contained both coconut and figs and that it was 'heaven on a plate'. This is my version...

Ingredients

For the Cake:
3 cups desiccated coconut

2 cups plain flour

4 teaspoons baking powder

200g butter

2 cups caster sugar

7 large eggs

50mL light olive oil

1 cup coconut threads, toasted (for toasting, refer to basics)

80g dried Greek figs, chopped

For the Syrup:

1 1/2 cups of sugar

juice and rind of 3 lemons

Method

1. Grease a 24cm square or round cake tin generously and coat with some of the desiccated coconut. Preheat the oven to 190°C.

2. Sift together the plain flour and baking powder.

3. Cream the butter and sugar until light and fluffy. With the motor running, add the eggs one at a time and beat well after each addition. Fold through the olive oil, coconut, toasted coconut threads, figs and flour mixture and combine thoroughly.

4. Pour into the prepared tin and bake at 190°C for 10 minutes, then reduce the heat to 150°C and bake for a further 65 minutes or until 'springy' when pressed gently on the surface.

5. Meanwhile, slice off the thin yellow exterior of the lemons and slice into strips. Boil the sugar, lemon strips and juice for 3 minutes and strain, reserving the strips for garnish.

6. When the cake has been removed from the oven, pour the syrup over the cake and allow the cake to cool.

7. Gently run a knife between the cake and the tin and remove the cake. Slice and serve, garnished with the caramelised strips of lemon rind.

Torta di Polenta *con* Limone
Lemon Polenta Cake

Polenta is made from dried corn, and is a speciality of the north of Italy, where it is served in a variety of ways. It is simmered, baked, fried, grilled and, of course, used as an ingredient in cakes and pies. This is one of my favourite recipes and the inspiration here came from a little trattoria in Trento in Italy's north, where I had a moist, tender polenta cake as a reward after a brisk bush walk.

Ingredients

500g butter, softened

500g caster sugar

zest and juice of 3 lemons

zest and juice of 1 orange

6 large eggs

2 teaspoons vanilla essence

500g almond meal

300g yellow polenta

2 teaspoons baking powder

icing sugar, to serve

Lemon Marscapone:

500g marscapone cheese

1 cup of icing sugar

juice of 1 lemon

Method

1. Preheat the oven to 170°C and butter a 24cm springform non-stick cake tin.

2. Beat the butter, sugar and zests of lemon and orange together until thick and pale. With the motor running, add the eggs, one at a time and beat well after each addition.

3. Remove the bowl from the mixer, then mix in the lemon juice, orange juice, vanilla essence, almond meal, polenta and baking powder. Mix thoroughly so that all the ingredients are combined.

4. Pour the batter into the prepared tin, tapping gently to make sure there are no air bubbles.

5. Bake at 170°C for 1 hour, then reduce the heat to 160°C and bake for a further 40 minutes. If necessary, cover the cake with foil if it is beginning to brown too quickly.

6. When the cake is finished baking, remove it from the oven and allow it to cool in the tin. When it is cold, remove the cake from the tin.

7. To serve, sprinkle with icing sugar and serve with some lemon spiked marscapone (recipe follows).

Lemon Marscapone:

To make this creamy accompaniment, beat the cheese, sugar and lemon juice together until smooth then chill until ready to serve.

Greek Rum *and* Hazelnut Cake

This richly flavoured cake is usually served after a large and spicy meal, to encourage 'sweetness' in one's life. One of my Greek friends gave me a version of this recipe which she watched her grandmother make many times during her childhood. She now bakes it for her children to carry on the tradition. You needn't worry about children becoming drunk on the rum – the alcohol is evaporated during the cooking of the syrup!

Ingredients

For the Cake:

500g toasted hazelnuts

100g plain sweet biscuits

2 teaspoons baking powder

zest of 1 lemon

8 large eggs, separated

1/4 teaspoon cream of tartar

1 cup sugar

135g butter, melted

100g whole roasted hazelnuts, roughly crushed

For the Syrup:

1 cup sugar

1/2 cup water

1/3 cup dark rum

Method

1. In a food processor, blend together the hazelnuts and biscuits until finely ground. Add the baking powder and zest and pulse briefly.

2. Beat the egg whites with the cream of tartar until soft peaks form, then continue beating while adding 4 tablespoons sugar, one at a time. Once the sugar has been added and dissolved, the whites should be stiff and glossy.

3. In a clean bowl, beat together the egg yolks and remaining sugar until the mixture is thick and pale.

4. Fold the nut mixture into the yolks, then add the melted butter and stir thoroughly to combine.

5. Pour the cake batter on top of the whites and gently fold together using a spatula.

6. Spoon the cake batter into a greased and floured 30cm x 20cm cake tin or metal baking dish then sprinkle the remaining nuts over the top.

7. Bake at 180°C for 40 minutes or until no longer 'wobbly' in the centre.

8. Meanwhile, make the rum syrup. Bring the sugar and water to the boil and simmer for five minutes. Add the rum and continue boiling for three more minutes then set aside to cool.

9. When the cake has finished cooking, remove from the oven and pour over the warm syrup. Allow to cool then cut into diamond shapes (like baklava). Serve with a little extra syrup drizzled over.

Note: The easiest way to cut a rectangular cake into diamonds is as follows: First, cut three or four strips of cake from one end of the tin to the other. Then, hold your knife at a 45 degree angle and cut further strips diagonally across the tin.

Torta Tiramisù

This Italian torta is a relatively new addition to the cake world and has become an instant celebrity. It is quite different from the pudding-like Tiramisù that graces most Italian restaurant dessert menus at the moment, but is just as delicious. It is definitely more elegant to serve at a formal occasion because it slices so beautifully. This recipe is best made one day before serving.

Ingredients

For the Meringue:

pinch of salt

6 egg whites

230g caster sugar

100g roasted almonds, ground

40g cornflour

20g icing sugar

For the Custard Filling:

7 level teaspoons gelatine

60mL water

125mL coffee liqueur

125g caster sugar

60g instant coffee

500g marscapone cheese

4 egg yolks

250mL thickened (double or heavy) cream, whipped

100g finely grated Lindt or Saraotti dark chocolate

cocoa powder for dusting

Method

1. Preheat the oven to 180°C. Grease and line two 24cm springform tins.

2. Firstly, make the meringue bases. Beat the egg whites and salt until stiff peaks form and then gradually add the caster sugar, a little at a time. Beat at top speed for 10 minutes until the sugar is completely dissolved and the mixture is thick and glossy.

3. In a separate bowl, mix the almonds, icing sugar and cornflour, then gently fold into the egg white mixture. Divide the mixture evenly between the cake tins and bake at 180°C for 45 minutes, then cool completely before using. (If you do not have two 24cm cake tins, bake half the mixture and when cool, remove from the tin. Re-grease and line the cake tin to bake the remaining mixture.)

4. Place the gelatine and water in a small bowl and stand in a pan of boiling water to dissolve, or heat in a microwave oven on 'high' for ten seconds. Place the coffee liqueur, sugar and instant coffee in a saucepan and bring to the boil. Stir in the dissolved gelatine and mix well. Set aside. Place the marscapone in a mixing bowl and beat in the egg yolks and coffee mixture. Gently fold in the whipped cream and mix gently.

To assemble the cake:
Place one of the meringue bases in the bottom of a 23cm (9") springform pan and pour half the marscapone mixture. Smooth then sprinkle with half the grated chocolate. Top with the second base and press down lightly. Cover with remaining marscapone mixture and remaining chocolate. Chill for at least 2 hours. Carefully remove from the sides of the cake tin, then slide the cake off the base. Dust the top of the cake with cocoa powder.

Variation: To make a rectangular torta, follow the above recipe but use a long, rectangular loaf tin to bake and assemble the cake.

Torta *di* Riso
Italian Rice Cake

The recipe for this traditional peasant style cake came about as a result of several trips to Italy where I was charmed by the taste of individual rice cakes, served mid-morning with very strong coffee at Italy's famous espresso bars. The flavours of a cake made from an ingredient as simple as rice still amaze me. Even the pastry uses rice as its main ingredient.

Ingredients

120g rice flour

130g plain flour

50g pistachio kernels

70g brown sugar

100g white sugar

220g butter

2 large eggs

750mL milk

160g Vialone Nano rice

4 egg yolks

zest of 1 large lemon

2 tablespoons chopped blanched almonds

1/4 teaspoon ground nutmeg

1/4 teaspoon ground cinnamon

Method

1 Process the rice flour, plain flour, pistachio nuts and a pinch of salt together until the nuts are roughly chopped. Add the brown sugar, 120g butter and 1 egg, briefly in a food processor, until combined. Remove the dough and knead briefly until smooth. Cover and refrigerate for a minimum of thirty minutes.

2 Place the milk and rice in a saucepan with a pinch of salt and simmer for 30 minutes, or until the rice is tender and milk has been absorbed. Set aside.

3 In a separate bowl, combine 75g of white sugar, 50g of remaining butter, 4 egg yolks, lemon zest, almonds and mix well. Stir the mixture into the rice, making sure that the ingredients are well combined.

4 Roll out the pastry to 5mm thick and place over the base and sides of a buttered 22cm springform cake tin with a removable base. Gently press the pastry into the tin, patching any areas that tear. Make sure the pastry reaches the top edge of the cake tin.

5 Pour the rice mixture into the pastry case. Combine remaining egg, remaining butter, remaining 25g of white sugar, nutmeg and cinnamon and mix well. Drizzle over the surface of the cake.

6 Bake the cake at 180°C for one hour or until cooked through and golden. Allow to cool in the tin, then gently remove the sides of the cake tin. Serve with cream if desired.

Sicilian Torta *di* Mele
Apple Cake from Sicily

This is an easy cake that any Italian 'mama' would be proud of. The simple ingredients combine to produce a delicious cake that is full of flavour and just as good served warm or cool.

Ingredients

120g butter, melted

50g toasted walnuts, ground

1kg Granny Smith apples

zest and juice of 1 lemon

3 large eggs

2 teaspoons vanilla essence

250g sugar

150g flour

2 teaspoons baking powder

100mL milk

120g raisins

100g pine nuts, toasted

3 tablespoons sugar

1 teaspoon cinnamon

1 tablespoon icing sugar

Method

1 Preheat the oven to 190°C.

2 Using 20g of butter from the total quantity, grease a 24cm cake tin generously, then sprinkle with the ground walnuts. Set aside.

3 Peel and core and quarter the apples, then cut them into slices. Toss the apples with the zest and juice of the lemon and set aside.

4 Whisk the eggs, vanilla and sugar together until pale and creamy, then add the melted butter, flour, baking powder and milk. Mix thoroughly.

5 Pour one third of the batter into the prepared cake tin, then top with one third of apple, raisins and pine nuts. Repeat with remaining ingredients, then finish with layer of apples, then sprinkle the combined sugar and cinnamon over the top.

6 Bake at 190°C for 55 minutes, then allow to cool in the tin for 20 minutes. Unmould and sprinkle with icing sugar before serving.

Turkish *Tatlisi*
Lemon Yoghurt Cake

Syrup cakes feature heavily in Mediterranean and Middle Eastern countries. This version has the unmistakable tang of yoghurt which provides a refreshing quality. The aromatic lemon syrup finishes this cake off beautifully.

Ingredients

250g butter

1 1/4 cups caster sugar

zest of 2 lemons

5 large eggs, separated

1 1/4 cups Greek style yoghurt

2 1/2 cups self raising flour

1/2 teaspoon salt

1 cup of sugar

3/4 cup water

juice of two lemons

rind of two lemons, cut into fine strips

1 cup thick cream, flavoured with cinnamon or nutmeg, for serving

Method

1 Preheat the oven to 175°C.

2 Cream together the butter, sugar and lemon zest until thick and fluffy. Reduce the mixing speed to low and add the egg yolks, one at a time. Finally, add the yoghurt and mix well.

3 Add the flour and salt to the batter and mix to incorporate.

4 Beat the egg whites until stiff, then fold into the batter gently.

5 Pour the batter into a greased 'Kugelhopf' or tube pan and bake for 50–60 minutes.

6 Meanwhile, make the syrup. Mix together the sugar, water, lemon juice and rind and bring to the boil. Simmer for 10 minutes, then cool. Strain syrup through a sieve, reserving strips of lemon, then set aside.

7 When the cake has cooked, pour syrup over the cake slowly, allowing it to absorb into the cake. When all the syrup has been absorbed and the cake is cool, turn out onto a platter to serve

8 Serve the cake, decorated with the reserved lemon strips and with thick cream, flavoured with cinnamon or nutmeg.

The Cakes of Europe

Cakes have been an important part of European cuisine for centuries. Every country and region has its own favourites, and with Europe being as diverse as it is, you can imagine that this chapter will reach only the 'tip of the iceberg'.

We have included recipes rich in tradition, with all the flavours of Eastern Europe. These cakes tend to be dense and full flavoured and keep very well.

Deliciously satisfying cakes from Austria, Switzerland and other European countries that use chocolate, fruit, spices, cheese and cream. Cakes based on flavourful batters that rise well, pastry designed to crumble, crowning rich and sweet fruit fillings.

We have chosen not to include cakes that take hours of preparation, like French tortes and gateaux, because this book is devoted to delicious cakes that are quick and easy to make and will guarantee you great results every time.

Danish Plum Prune Batter *Cake*

Cakes such as this one evoke memories of long winter nights, open fireplaces and nurturing
family gatherings. I am a great fan of cakes with crunchy toppings and this one is a real favourite.
By making use of the food processor, this cake is simplicity itself!

Ingredients

For the Cake:

200g caster sugar

90g self raising flour

1 teaspoon baking powder

150g butter

2 large eggs

½ cup milk

1 teaspoon vanilla essence

For the Topping:

10 stoned prunes

6 hard plums, stoned and quartered

130g shelled walnuts or pecans

60g demerara sugar

1 teaspoon cinnamon

40g butter

Method

1 Preheat the oven to 190°C and butter a 26cm non-stick springform cake tin.

2 In a food processor, place the sugar, flour and baking powder and 'pulse' for a few seconds to aerate. Add the butter, eggs, milk and vanilla and process until the batter is smooth – about 20 seconds, scraping down the sides of the bowl.

3 Pour the batter into the cake tin, then dot with the prunes and plum pieces. Mix together the walnuts, sugar and cinnamon and sprinkle this mixture over the fruit. Dot with the butter.

4 Bake at 190°C for one hour or until golden brown and crisp.

5 Serve warm with a little thick cream, flavoured with nutmeg if you like.

Austrian Maple Spice *Cake* (photographed on page 29)

This is one of the most delicious cakes I have eaten. The cake itself is moist and flavoursome and is crowned by a rich chocolate glaze over a thin layer of marmalade in the tradition of 'Sacher Torte', the famous Austrian cake created by the Hotel Sacher. This cake makes a perfect gift for your loved ones.

Ingredients

For the Cake:

3 cups of self raising flour

2 tablespoons cinnamon

1 teaspoon ground cloves

2 teaspoons ground ginger

2 tablespoons Dutch cocoa

1 cup of pure maple syrup

½ cup of honey

1 ½ cups of caster sugar

1 ½ cups of buttermilk

1 teaspoon pure vanilla extract

For the Glaze:

200g cooking chocolate

2 tablespoons butter

juice and rind of one small orange

3 tablespoons marmalade or apricot jam

4 tablespoons sugar

2 teaspoons water

Method

1 Butter a non-stick 28cm or 26cm springform tin and set aside. Preheat the oven to 180°C.

2 In a large bowl, mix together the flour, cinnamon, ground cloves, ginger and cocoa. In a separate bowl, whisk the maple syrup, honey, sugar, buttermilk and vanilla. Gently but thoroughly combine the flour mixture and the syrup mixture.

3 Pour the batter into the prepared cake tin and bake at 170°C for 1 hour and 10 minutes, until the cake is 'springy' when pressed gently in the centre. Remove the cake from the oven and cool thoroughly in the tin.

4 When the cake is cold, remove it from the cake tin and set aside.

5 To make the glaze, melt the chocolate and butter, either in the microwave or in a bowl resting over a saucepan of simmering water. When melted, whisk in the orange juice thoroughly.

6 Meanwhile, warm the marmalade and gently spread it over the surface of the cake. Allow to cool.

7 When the chocolate mixture is smooth, carefully pour it over the marmalade topped cake and spread to cover.

8 Cut the rind of the orange into fine strips or use a 'zester'.

9 Heat the sugar and water together in a small saucepan and, when liquid, add the orange strips and simmer for 5 minutes. Lift out the caramelised orange strips and allow to cool. (Discard remaining syrup.)

10 Before serving, pile the caramelised orange strips in the centre of the cake.

Russian *Cheesecake*

The cheesecakes of Eastern European Jewry have a reputation for being the most delicious in the world. They are not light and fluffy like so many modern versions, but dense, full of flavour and texture. This recipe is a family 'heirloom', given to me in part by my grandmother, and then completed by a Russian aunt many years later.

Ingredients

For the Crust:

3 tablespoons sugar

3 tablespoons brown sugar

1/2 teaspoon nutmeg

3 tablespoons butter, softened

3/4 cup ground walnuts

3/4 cup plain flour

1 teaspoon baking powder

For the Cheesecake:

700g creamed cheese, softened

200g soft white cheese such as ricotta

1 1/2 cups of sugar

6 large eggs, separated

juice and zest of 1 large lemon

3 tablespoons plain flour

1 cup of thick cream

1 cup of sultanas (optional)

2 tablespoons icing sugar

Method

1. Preheat the oven to 200°C and butter a 28cm non-stick springform cake tin. Remove the base of the cake tin from the sides and lay a piece baking paper over the base. Replace the sides to hold the paper in place.

2. First, prepare the crust. Using a food processor or blender, pulse together all the 'crust' ingredients until a stiff dough forms. Roll out the dough and press over the base of the cake tin. Bake at 200°C for 10 minutes then remove from the oven and cool.

3. Meanwhile, in a large bowl of an electric mixer, combine the creamed cheese, white cheese and 1 cup of sugar and beat for 3 minutes or until the mixture is smooth. Add the egg yolks one at a time, beating well after each addition. Add the juice and zest of the lemon and the plain flour, and mix until combined.

4. In a separate bowl, beat the egg whites until foaming, then add the remaining half cup of sugar, sprinkling the sugar into the egg whites while the motor is running. When all the sugar has been added, raise the speed of the mixer to the fastest, then allow the egg whites to beat until they are thick and glossy.

5. In a separate bowl, beat the cream until soft peaks form.

6. Fold the beaten cream and the egg whites into the cheese mixture and combine thoroughly. Pour the batter into the cooled crust, then sprinkle the sultanas over the batter and gently stir a few in so that they drop below the surface.

7. Bake at 200°C for 10 minutes, then reduce the heat to 150°C and cook for an hour. Turn off the oven heat and leave the cake in the oven undisturbed. When the cake has cooled, remove from the oven and chill overnight.

8. Transfer the cake to a platter then gently ease the paper out from under the cake.

9. Sprinkle with icing sugar and serve.

English Syrup Sour Cream *Cake*

The English are famous for their range of warming winter puddings and I came across a similar recipe to this one, quite by chance, when looking through some very old cookbooks. I have modernised some of the ingredients and the method, without changing the flavours of this delicious country cake.

Ingredients

200g soft butter

200g caster sugar

1 teaspoon vanilla essence

3 eggs

1 apple, peeled and grated

200g self raising flour

50g plain flour

100g sour cream

5 tablespoons golden syrup

5 tablespoons golden syrup, extra

fresh fruit and custard
or cream for serving

Method

1 Preheat the oven to 190°C and butter a 20cm cake tin (not springform). Line the base of the tin with baking paper, allowing the paper to come up the sides a little. Press the paper to the sides of the tin.

2 Cream the butter and sugar together, then add the vanilla and eggs, one at a time and beating well after each addition. Add the grated apple, then the combined flours and sour cream, beating well to combine all the ingredients thoroughly until the mixture is smooth.

3 Pour the golden syrup into the base of the prepared cake tin, then spoon the cake batter over the top.

4 Cover the cake tin with a large piece of buttered foil, buttered side down towards the cake batter and secure the foil with string around the edge of the cake tin.

5 Place the cake tin in a large baking dish and add hot water until it reaches halfway up the side of the cake tin.

6 Bake at 190°C for 75 minutes, then remove the cake tin from the water and allow to cool for 20 minutes before turning out onto a cake platter.

7 Heat the extra golden syrup, then pour over the top of the cake and serve with some fresh fruit of your choice, and some custard or cream.

Flourless Poppyseed *Cake*

I grew up on cakes made with poppyseed – an Eastern European speciality, particularly loved by European Jews. The poppyseeds are always minced or ground prior to baking and this can be done for you by many European style delicatessens. To do it yourself, simply weigh the amount you need, then grind in a food processor, coffee grinder or mortar and pestle.

Ingredients

4 large eggs, separated

125g butter

grated rind of 1 lemon

100g icing sugar

2 tablespoons Dutch cocoa

50g caster sugar

160g poppy seeds

extra icing sugar to serve

Method

1 Preheat the oven to 170°C and butter a 24cm round cake tin. Set aside.

2 In the bowl of an electric mixer, beat the egg yolks, soft butter, grated lemon rind and icing sugar until thick and smooth, about 5 minutes. Fold in the cocoa and mix well.

3 Meanwhile, beat the egg whites until 'foamy', raise the speed and sprinkle in the caster sugar while the eggs are beating. Continue until the egg whites are thick and glossy.

4 Mix the poppyseeds into the yolk mixture, then add the egg whites and combine gently.

5 Spoon the batter into the prepared tin and smooth the top.

6 Bake at 170°C for 70 minutes. Remove the cake from the oven and allow to cool in the tin.

7 When the cake is cold, remove from the tin and dust with icing sugar. For a more decorative finish, cut strips of paper and lay these over the cake before dusting with icing sugar.

Variation: My children love this cake iced with a simple chocolate glaze. To try this, mix together 1 cup of icing sugar, 2 tablespoons cocoa and 1–2 tablespoons boiling water. Mix well until thick and syrupy (adding more water if necessary), then spread over the cake and allow to cool and set.

Chocolate Sand *Cake*

This Hungarian cake is so-named because of the texture of the cake's exterior once it is baked. The addition of chocolate is a little artistic licence on my part; it increases the flavour and adds a lovely texture.

Ingredients

50g sweet biscuit crumbs

200g butter or margarine

6 eggs

1/2 cup of sugar

1/2 cup of brown sugar

2 cups of plain flour

1 tablespoon baking powder

3 tablespoons cocoa

80mL milk

1 teaspoon vanilla extract

1 cup of mixed dried fruit (or 1 cup of any single variety of dried fruit, e.g. sultanas, currants etc.)

Method

1 Generously butter a non-stick fluted cake tin and sprinkle the biscuit crumbs all over the buttered area. Set aside. Preheat the oven to 170°C.

2 Slowly melt the butter or margarine. Meanwhile, using an electric mixer, beat the eggs and sugars together until the mixture is very thick and pale, about 8 minutes. With the motor still running, add the melted butter to the egg mixture in a thin stream and continue beating until all the ingredients are combined.

3 In a separate bowl, mix the flour, baking powder and cocoa together.

4 Combine the egg mixture, the flour mixture, the vanilla extract and the milk with a wooden spoon, continuing to mix until the batter is smooth. Add the dried fruit and mix briefly to distribute.

5 Pour the batter into the prepared tin, then bake the cake at 170°C for 40 minutes. Allow to cool for a few minutes in the tin, then turn out onto a wire rack and cool.

6 Dust with a little icing sugar or cocoa if desired.

Viennese Apple Sour Cream *Cake*

This delicious dessert cake is full of apples, with a streusel-type filling that absorbs the apple juices and holds the cake together. The base can be made with any sweet biscuits but I like to use ginger snaps to bring out the flavours of the apples. Serve the cake warm with thick cream or ice cream.

Ingredients

For the Base:

190g ginger snap biscuits

pinch of cinnamon

80g melted butter

For the Filling:

1.5kg Granny Smith apples

200g brown sugar

100g plain flour

1/2 teaspoon cinnamon

1/2 teaspoon allspice

1/2 cup sultanas or currants

For the Topping:

300mL sour cream

2 tablespoons icing sugar

For Serving:

icing sugar (cinnamon flavoured), to taste

Method

1. Preheat the oven to 180°C and butter a 24cm springform tin that has been lined with baking paper.

2. First, make the base. Process the biscuits and cinnamon together until fine crumbs and mix with the melted butter until the crumbs are all moistened. Press into the base of the prepared cake tin, compacting with the aid of a potato masher if necessary. Peel and slice the apples thinly and set aside. Process the flour, brown sugar and spices together and set aside.

3. Place a third of the apples over the crumb base, then sprinkle with the currants or sultanas. Sprinkle 2 tablespoons of the flour mixture over the fruit, tapping the tin to allow the excess to fall between the fruit pieces. Repeat these layers of apple, sultanas and flour mixture until all ingredients are used, ending with the sprinkling of flour mixture.

4. Mix the sour cream with the icing sugar and spread evenly over the cake. Bake at 180°C for 45 minutes, then remove the cake from the oven and chill overnight. Remove the cake from the tin and dredge with icing sugar flavoured with sprinkles of cinnamon. Serve warm or cold.

Swiss Apple Crumble *Cake*

This cake is a real 'rustic' version of traditional Swiss apple cakes. My father has spent many years in Switzerland and, while visiting him, I was treated to many versions of crumble cakes with various fruit fillings. Although the addition of cheese may seem unusual, it is a traditional ingredient in many apple cakes. This cake is my own creation – an amalgam of all those I enjoyed and a tribute to those wonderfully capable Swiss bakers.

Ingredients

For the Cake:

600g Granny Smith Apples

80g sultanas

50g raisins

100g hazelnut kernels, toasted and chopped

200g self raising flour

1 teaspoon baking powder

80g brown sugar

50g rolled oats

2 teaspoons mixed spice

3 eggs

80g butter, melted

50g grated Jarlsberg cheese

For the Crumble:

80g sugar

80g plain flour

80g butter, softened

30g desiccated coconut

icing sugar, for dusting

Method

1. Butter a 24cm deep flan tin or springform cake tin and set aside. Preheat the oven to 200°C.

2. Peel and roughly dice the apples and toss with the sultanas, raisins and hazelnuts.

3. Mix together the self raising flour, baking powder, brown sugar, oats and mixed spice. In a separate bowl, whisk together the eggs and melted butter.

4. In a large bowl, mix together the apple mixture, flour mixture and egg mixture until thoroughly combined.

5. Pour half this mixture into the prepared tin, then sprinkle the cheese over. Spoon the remaining cake mixture over the cheese, taking care that all the cheese is covered.

6. In a small bowl, mix together the sugar, flour, butter and coconut until crumbly, then crumble this over the prepared cake mixture.

7. Bake at 200°C for 1 hour, then lower the heat to 160°C and bake for a further 30 minutes or until the top is golden, dry and crisp. Serve warm, dusted with icing sugar.

Variation: This cake works very well with other firm fruits such as pears and hard blood plums. Use the same amount of fruit as above and follow the recipe.

The Cakes of the Middle East

*T*he Middle East region includes countries like Israel, Syria, Lebanon and Egypt and, while testing these recipes, my kitchen began to smell a lot like an Middle Eastern market – rich with spices, roasting nuts and other delicious aromas.

The cakes in this chapter will surprise and delight you. They tend to be full of interesting textures and ingredients, so that every mouthful brings new flavours.

I am sure that any of these recipes will be quite at home after a rich and spicy Middle Eastern dinner, or even just because you deserve a treat!

Middle Eastern Glacé Fruit *Cake*

The Middle Eastern countries are known for their love of sweet and sticky treats and glacé fruits feature highly in most Jewish and Arab markets. I developed this recipe when a favourite Aunt gave me a huge tray of glacé apricots – far more than even the most avid eater could consume. The flavours of apricot and orange marry beautifully and the almond cake base is dense enough to carry such a heavy topping

Ingredients

250g butter, softened

250g sugar

grated zest and juice of two oranges

4 large eggs

400g blanched almonds, toasted and ground

1 cup of flour

½ cup of fine semolina

4 teaspoons baking powder

200g glacé apricots, half chopped and half sliced

2 cups sugar

1 cup water

5 tablespoons boiling water

2 tablespoons orange marmalade, heated and strained

1 cup creme fraîche or yoghurt, flavoured with orange or cinnamon, for serving

Method

1 Generously butter a lined 24cm springform cake tin and preheat the oven to 175°C.

2 Cream together the butter, sugar and orange zest until thick and pale. Add the eggs, one at a time and beat well after each addition. Fold in the ground almonds and orange juice.

3 Mix together the flour, semolina and baking powder and add to the cake batter with the chopped glacé apricots. Mix thoroughly.

4 Spoon the batter into the prepared tin and bake at 175°C for 50 minutes or until cooked through.

5 Meanwhile, make the topping by bringing the sugar and water to the boil. Simmer until deep golden brown, then remove from the heat. Carefully add the boiling water (be careful because the toffee might splatter); stir thoroughly. Add the strained marmalade and set aside.

6 Remove the cake from the oven and allow to cool in the tin for 10 minutes, then turn out onto a wire rack. Pile the remaining sliced glacé apricots over the cake and pour over the marmalade syrup.

7 Serve warm or cool with some creme fraîche or yoghurt, flavoured with orange and cinnamon.

Sephardi Carrot Cake (photographed on page 45)

The 'Sephardim' are those Jews who have lived in and around the Middle Eastern Arab countries and Europe since the late 15th century after being expelled from Spain (at that time a Muslim country). The Jews of German descent who migrated to the Middle East are called 'Ashkenazim'. This carrot cake has many interesting flavours that have been adapted over the years into the Sephardi diet and is healthy as well as flavoursome.

Ingredients

2 cups of caster sugar

8 eggs, separated

zest of 2 lemons

3 cups of raw grated carrot

4 cups of ground almonds

1 cup of self raising flour

2 teaspoons cinnamon

1 cup walnuts, toasted

1/2 cup raisins

1/2 teaspoon salt

2 tablespoons Israeli peach jam or marmalade

1 tablespoon boiling water

icing sugar, for dusting

Method

1. Grease a 26cm round springform cake tin and set aside. Preheat the oven to 190°C.

2. Beat the sugar, egg yolks and lemon zest together until thick and creamy. Fold in the grated carrot and ground almonds by hand until thoroughly mixed, then add the self raising flour, cinnamon, walnuts and raisins.

3. Beat the egg whites with the salt until stiff and then fold into the cake batter gently.

4. Spoon the cake batter into the prepared pan and bake at 190°C for 45–50 minutes or until firm.

5. Turn the cake out of the tin. Mix the jam with boiling water until smooth, then brush over cake.

6. When cool, dust with icing sugar and serve.

Israeli Pecan Date *Cake*

This lovely, nutty cake is not too sweet and I like to serve it for morning or afternoon tea. It keeps very well and makes a lovely dessert if 'zapped' in the microwave and served with vanilla bean ice-cream.

Ingredients

2 large eggs

180mL honey

150mL buttermilk

1 teaspoon vanilla essence

3 mashed bananas

2 cups of self raising flour

1 teaspoon baking powder

½ cup packed brown sugar

2 tablespoons Dutch cocoa

1 teaspoon cinnamon

1 teaspoon allspice

¼ teaspoon salt

125mL butter, very soft

1 cup 'Californian' dates* pitted (see note), chopped

1 cup pecan halves, toasted

2 tablespoons honey

Method

1. Preheat the oven to 170°C and generously butter a non-stick, 22cm springform cake tin.

2. In a bowl, mix together the eggs, honey, buttermilk and vanilla essence until smooth. Add the mashed bananas and set aside.

3. Reserve two tablespoons of flour and then, in a large bowl, mix together remaining flour, baking powder, brown sugar, cocoa, cinnamon, allspice and salt.

4. Using an electric mixer if possible (or a large bowl and spoon) place the flour mixture in the mixer bowl and add the liquid mixture. Mix gently until the ingredients are moistened, then add the butter and continue beating on medium to high speed until the batter is smooth, about 4 minutes.

5. Mix the reserved two tablespoons of the flour with the pitted chopped dates and pecan nuts, then fold this mixture into the cake batter.

6. Spoon the batter into the prepared tin and bake for 1 hour and 20 minutes. When ready, the cake should yield slightly to pressure when gently pressed in the centre of the top. Remove the cake from the oven and heat the remaining two tablespoons of honey. Brush this honey over the cake and then leave the cake to cool.

7. When cool, carefully remove from the tin and serve within 5 days, dusted with icing sugar if desired.

Note: The Californian dates called for in this recipe are large, soft dates, available from most good quality green grocers. If you cannot find them, use the same amount of a Middle Eastern brand.

Syrian Halva *Cake*

Halva is a Middle Eastern confectionery with a sweet flavour and gritty texture. This cake has a similar texture and flavour, developed by combining the wholemeal flour with ground nuts and sugar. The cake tin is coated in ground halva and then small chunks are added to the cake, giving it a thoroughly delicious flavour.

Ingredients

120g halva (available from Middle Eastern stores)

1 cup of raw sugar

3 tablespoons brown sugar

250g soft butter

zest of an orange

zest of a lemon

4 large eggs, separated

1 cup of semolina

1 cup of wholemeal flour

1 teaspoon cinnamon

½ teaspoon ground cloves

4 teaspoons baking powder

150mL milk

500g walnuts, coarsely chopped

3 tablespoons ground almonds

1 cup of sugar

1 cup of water

1 tablespoon orange flower water

icing sugar, for sprinkling

Method

1. Weigh the halva and remove 20g. Crush this finely and coarsely chop the remainder.

2. Preheat the oven to 190°C and butter a non-stick fluted 'kugelhopf' cake tin, sprinkling the finely ground halva over the greased cake tin. Tip the tin to coat evenly.

3. In a mixer, beat the raw sugar, brown sugar, butter and zests of lemon and orange together until thick and pale. Add the egg yolks one at a time, beating well after each addition.

4. In a separate bowl, mix together the semolina, wholemeal flour, cinnamon, ground cloves and baking powder. Add this flour mix to the butter batter, alternating with the milk.

5. Add the chopped walnuts, ground almonds and chopped halva and mix well.

6. Beat the egg whites until stiff peaks form, then fold into the cake batter gently.

7. Spoon the mixture into the prepared cake tin and bake for 40–50 minutes until firm.

8. Meanwhile, boil the sugar and water for 5 minutes, then add the orange flower water and set aside.

9. When the cake is removed from the oven, pour the flower water syrup over the cake and allow to cool. Remove the cake from the tin carefully and serve, generously sprinkled with icing sugar.

Syrian Nut *Cake*

This crunchy cake is full of interesting flavours and textures. Although alcohol is not allowed in a Muslim country, I like to brush a brandy flavoured syrup over this cake as it cools. This cake keeps very well and is lovely served warm with ice-cream. The easiest way to prepare the nuts is to toast them in the microwave or oven until golden, then 'pulse' in a food processor until well chopped but not finely ground.

Ingredients

125g butter

zest of 1 lemon

1 cup sugar

5 large eggs, separated

1 1/2 cups plain flour

1 tablespoon baking powder

1 teaspoon cinnamon

1/2 teaspoon ground cloves

1/2 teaspoon salt

1 cup finely chopped walnuts

1 cup finely chopped pistachio nuts

1/2 cup toasted slivered or flaked almonds

1 1/2 cups sugar

1 cup water

juice of 1 lemon

2 tablespoons brandy

icing sugar, for dusting

Method

1. Generously butter a 24cm springform cake tin and set aside. Preheat the oven to 170°C.

2. Cream the butter, lemon zest and 3/4 cup of the sugar until light and fluffy, then add the eggs yolks and beat well until combined.

3. With an electric mixer, whisk the egg whites until foaming, then add the remaining 1/4 cup sugar, one spoonful at a time, while still whisking. Continue whisking until the egg whites are thick, glossy and stiff.

4. Mix together the flour, baking powder, cinnamon, cloves and salt, then add this to the egg mixture.

5. Add the chopped and slivered nuts and mix well.

6. Add a large spoonful of the beaten egg whites and mix thoroughly, then fold in the remaining egg whites, taking care not to collapse the volume.

7. Spoon the batter into the prepared cake tin and bake at 170°C for 50–55 minutes.

8. Meanwhile, in a small saucepan bring to boil the sugar, water and lemon. Boil for 5 minutes, then add the brandy, simmer for 1 minute further, then set aside to cool slightly.

9. When the cake is baked, remove from the oven and brush with the prepared syrup. Leave the cake to cool in the tin, then turn out, dust with icing sugar and serve at room temperature.

Sweet Potato Date *Cake*

Dates are loved all over the Middle East. These sweet, sticky fruits are incredibly good for you and feature in so many recipes from this area of the world. Try to buy Israeli dates because they are bigger and more succulent than their Arab cousins.

Ingredients

600g sweet potato

250g butter, soft

300g sugar

4 eggs

300g self raising flour

1 teaspoon cinnamon

1 teaspoon nutmeg

14 dates, stones removed and flesh chopped

1 cup walnut halves, toasted

2 tablespoons honey

1/2 cup sugar

50mL water

1/2 teaspoon cinnamon, extra

icing sugar, for dusting

Method

1 Generously butter a fluted cake tin. Preheat the oven to 190°C.

2 Peel the sweet potato. Using a grater, grate 30 strips of sweet potato and set aside. Chop the remaining sweet potato and cover with water. Simmer until soft, then drain and mash or process until smooth. Set aside.

3 Beat the butter and sugar then add sweet potato. Add the eggs, one at a time and beat well after each addition.

4 Add the flour, cinnamon and nutmeg with chopped dates and walnuts and mix thoroughly.

5 Spoon the batter into the cake tin and bake at 190°C for 40 minutes until cooked through.

6 Meanwhile, simmer the strips of sweet potato in honey, sugar, water and extra cinnamon for 5 minutes. Lift out the caramelised strips and set aside.

7 Turn the cake out of the cake tin and allow to cool. Dust with icing sugar and top with the caramelised sweet potato strips.

Lebanese Tahina *Cake*

Tahina is sesame seed paste, similar in theory to natural peanut butter and, as a substitute, peanut butter works very well in this recipe. This cake has a rich, dense texture and makes a very good morning tea accompaniment. I like to bake this cake in a fluted cake tin, often called a kugelhopf tin.

Ingredients

3 tablespoons sesame seeds

1 cup of tahina (sesame seed paste)

3/4 cup caster sugar

1/4 cup brown sugar

grated rind and juice of two oranges

200g thick, plain yoghurt

2 1/2 cups self raising flour

1/2 teaspoon salt

1 teaspoon mixed spice

100g chopped pistachios

6 dates, stones removed and flesh chopped

3 tablespoons sesame seeds, additional

Method

1 Grease a 24cm cake tin generously and sprinkle with 3 tablespoons sesame seeds. Set aside. Preheat the oven to 170°C.

2 In the bowl of an electric mixer, beat the tahina, caster sugar, brown sugar and orange rind until thick and creamy. Add the orange juice and yoghurt. Continue to beat until combined.

3 Fold in the self raising flour, salt, mixed spice, pistachio nuts, sesame seeds and chopped dates and mix thoroughly by hand until all ingredients are well mixed and distributed.

4 Spoon the batter into the prepared cake tin and smooth the top.

5 Bake at 170°C for 45 minutes, or until cake is firm to the touch.

6 Turn the cake out of the tin and allow to cool.

The Cakes of the Americas

The Americas have an extensive tradition of cakes and baked goods that reflects the diverse nature of regions from Hawaii to Mexico, from Jamaica to the American heartlands.

In this chapter, we offer cakes that are modern, and some that have been around in one form or other for decades, if not centuries. Cakes that speak of the early days of American settlements and cakes that are modern and hip and very 'now'. In some recipes, we have taken the flavours of a certain region and created a recipe for a cake, that was never a cake before. For example, Florida is famous for Key Lime Pie, a kind of tangy Lemon Meringue Pie. Here, we offer you a recipe for Key Lime Cake, an interesting mix of flavours and textures that is easier to make than a pie, but just as delicious.

The things that all these cakes have in common – they are all scrumptious, easy to make and absolutely sure to make a big impression on your family and friends.

Jamaican Gingerbread *Cake*

This spicy cake is so versatile. It makes a lovely afternoon tea cake and is lovely warm for breakfast with honey or jam. But my favourite is to warm the cake and serve it 'sandwich-style' filled with rum and raisin ice-cream and fresh banana slices – this makes a superb winter dessert.

Ingredients

2 cups of self raising flour

2 teaspoons ground ginger

1 teaspoon fresh minced ginger

1 teaspoon cinnamon

1 teaspoon allspice

1/4 teaspoon nutmeg

1/4 teaspoon cloves

160g butter

3/4 cup packed brown sugar

1/2 cup molasses

1/2 cup honey

2 large eggs

3/4 cup sour cream

1 tablespoon vanilla essence

1 tablespoon lemon zest

thick pure cream, for serving

Method

1. Preheat the oven to 180°C and butter a loaf tin. Flour the tin lightly and set aside.

2. In a large bowl, mix together the flour, ginger, minced ginger, cinnamon, allspice, nutmeg and cloves and set aside.

3. In a mixer, cream together the butter, sugar, molasses and honey until thick and fluffy, then add the eggs, one at a time. When well mixed, remove the bowl from the mixer and add the sour cream, vanilla and lemon zest.

4. Add the dry flour mix and stir together gently but thoroughly with a wooden spoon. Pour the batter into the prepared tin and bake for 45 minutes. When cooked, the top of the cake should be golden brown and be slightly resistant to pressure when pressed gently on the top centre of the cake.

5. Remove the cake from the oven and cool in the tin. Serve in generous slices with thick cream as a mid meal snack or serve as a superb winter dessert (see introduction to this recipe).

Key Lime *Cake*

(photographed on page 59)

Florida is famous for 'Key Lime Pie', a deliciously tart pie, not too different from lemon meringue but with much more flavour. I have adapted my favourite key lime recipe to create this cake which keeps well and can be made with other varieties of lime. It is a lovely cake to serve when you want something refreshing and satisfying, all at once.

Ingredients

For the Cake:

100g pecan nuts, toasted and ground

250g butter, softened

2 cups of caster sugar

zest of 4 limes

5 large eggs

3 cups of self raising flour

100g ground almonds

1 cup milk

2 tablespoons chopped macadamia nuts, toasted

2 tablespoons sugar

For the Glaze:

juice of 4 limes

3/4 cup caster sugar

2 key limes

2 tablespoons coconut threads

Method

1. Preheat the oven to 180°C and generously butter a babka or fluted cake tin. Sprinkle the ground nuts over the buttered tin and set aside.

2. Cream together the butter, sugar and lime zest until light and fluffy. Add the eggs, one at a time and beat well after each addition.

3. Remove the bowl from the mixer and add the self raising flour, ground almonds and milk, and mix gently but thoroughly.

4. Mix together the macadamia nuts and sugar and sprinkle over the cake.

5. Bake the cake for 70 minutes or until golden and cooked through.

6. To make the glaze, whisk the lime juice and sugar together and heat gently until the sugar has dissolved. Slice the limes thinly and soak the limes in the lime syrup. Once the cake has finished baking, remove the cake from the oven and brush/pour the lime syrup all over the cake, continuing until it has all been absorbed. Allow the cake to cool in the tin.

7. When the cake has cooled and the syrup has been absorbed, decorate the cake with the lime slices and sprinkle with the coconut, then serve at room temperature.

Apple Cake *with* Maple Sauce

This delicious cake contains two ingredients that Americans love – apple sauce and maple syrup. American apple sauce is simply apple purée and it is used in everything from cakes to roast pork. I have adapted this cake from a Canadian recipe to create this rich and very satisfying dessert cake for you to share when you feel like a treat. If you cannot find apple purée, the baby food variety works very well.

Ingredients

For the Cake:

1 Granny Smith apple or
125mL apple purée

3 large Granny Smith apples, extra

375g self raising flour

1 teaspoon mixed spice

1/2 teaspoon nutmeg

2 cups of sugar

1/2 teaspoon salt

125g firm butter

3 large eggs

1/2 cup of peanut oil

2 teaspoons vanilla essence

For the Sauce:

250g Canadian maple syrup

125g thick cream

50g butter

good pinch of salt

ice cream

Method

1 Preheat the oven to 180°C and generously grease a babka tin or 20cm round tin with a central funnel. Dust with flour and set aside.

2 If you are using a fresh apple to make the purée, peel, core and chop the apple and simmer with 2 tablespoons water until very soft. Purée or fork mash the apple. Peel, core and dice the remaining three apples.

3 In a bowl, mix together the flour, mixed spice, nutmeg, sugar and salt. Rub the butter through with your fingertips until the mixture resembles fine breadcrumbs.

4 In a separate bowl, whisk together the eggs, oil and vanilla until smooth. Add the puréed apple and mix well. Using a wooden spoon, combine the flour mixture with the egg mixture, then fold in the diced apple pieces. Pour the batter into the prepared tin, then bake for 45–50 minutes or until golden and firm on top. Remove cake from the oven and allow to cool in the tin, then gently turn out.

5 For the syrup: Mix together the syrup, cream, butter and salt and bring to the boil. Simmer for 2 minutes then cool slightly. Serve the syrup spooned around the cake, with a scoop of vanilla ice-cream or some pure cream.

Mexican Chocolate *Cake*

Traditional Mexican cooks have been using chocolate for centuries. They add bitter chocolate to their chilli and mole sauces to give body and richness. Here, the Mexican love of chocolate is adapted to a rich, decadent dessert, topped with a milk chocolate ganache. Save this one for special occasions.

Ingredients

For the Cake:

2 cups of self raising flour

1 cup of Dutch cocoa powder

1 tablespoon cinnamon

375g butter, softened

2½ cups sugar

2 teaspoons vanilla essence

6 large eggs

3 tablespoons instant coffee powder

3 tablespoons hot water

1 cup buttermilk

For the Ganache:

125mL of thick cream

½ teaspoon cinnamon

1 tablespoon instant coffee powder

200g light chocolate, grated

For the Glaze:

150g dark chocolate, chopped

2 tablespoons butter

2 tablespoons corn syrup

Method

1. Preheat the oven to 180°C and butter a 28cm non-stick, springform cake tin, lining the base with baking paper.

2. Mix together the flour, cocoa, cinnamon and set aside.

3. Cream the butter and sugar together with the vanilla and beat until the mixture is thick and light. Add the eggs, one at a time, beating well after each addition.

4. In a jug, mix together the coffee powder with the hot water then add the buttermilk.

5. Using a wooden spoon or spatula, mix half the flour and buttermilk mixture into the creamed egg/sugar mixture and combine gently. Add the remaining flour and buttermilk mixtures and mix again.

6. Pour the batter into the prepared cake tin and bake for 55 minutes, until firm on top and 'bouncy' when you gently press the surface. Allow to cool then remove from the tin.

7. To make the Ganache, simmer together the cream, cinnamon and coffee powder, then pour this hot mixture over the grated chocolate. Allow to sit for a few minutes then stir gently to combine. Allow to cool. When cool, spread the ganache over the top of the cake then chill. For the glaze, place the chopped chocolate, butter and corn syrup in a bowl over simmering water and mix until smooth. Allow to cool a little, then gently drizzle over the ganache, covering it entirely. Chill the cake, then allow to come to room temperature before serving.

Louisiana Banana *Cake*

In America, a cake is not a cake unless it is topped with 'frosting', usually a butter and sugar concoction that is whipped together, then flavoured or coloured. Here, the frosting is heavily flavoured with banana and rum and then drenched in shredded coconut.

Ingredients

For the Cake:

2 cups of plain flour

1/4 cup cornflour

2 teaspoons baking powder

1 teaspoon baking soda

1/2 teaspoon nutmeg

200g butter, softened

1 cup of brown sugar

3 eggs

2 teaspoons vanilla essence

3/4 cup buttermilk

3 medium bananas, mashed

1/2 cup toasted pine nuts

1/2 cup shredded coconut

For the Frosting:

200g butter

3 cups icing sugar

2 small ripe bananas, mashed

125mL dark rum

1/2 teaspoon cinnamon

1 tablespoon vanilla essence

1 tablespoon fresh lemon juice

1 1/2 cups toasted shredded coconut

Method

1. Preheat the oven to 190°C and butter a 24cm springform, non-stick cake tin (or 23 x 13cm loaf tin).

2. In a large bowl, combine the flour, cornflour, baking powder, baking soda and nutmeg. Set aside.

3. Beat the butter and sugar together until light and fluffy, then add the eggs and vanilla essence and mix thoroughly. In a separate bowl, mix the buttermilk and mashed bananas.

4. Add half the flour mixture to the creamed sugar, then add half the buttermilk/banana mixture. Mix thoroughly, then add the remaining flour mixture and buttermilk/banana mixture and mix very well. Add the pine nuts and coconut and stir to distribute.

5. Pour the batter into the prepared cake tin and bake for 50 minutes, or until the cake is 'springy' in the centre when gently pressed. Remove the cake from the oven and cool in the tin for 30 minutes, then remove the cake from the tin and cool completely.

6. To make the frosting, beat the softened butter and icing sugar together until thick and pale, then fold through the bananas, rum, cinnamon, vanilla and lemon juice. Beat well to combine, then spread over the top of the cooled cake. Generously sprinkle the coconut over the cake, covering the frosting thoroughly.

New York Chocolate *Cake*

This superbly rich chocolate cake reminds me of a cake I enjoyed at the Palm Court at the Plaza Hotel in New York. The ambience of the magnificent surroundings made this afternoon (and the memory of the cake) more special. I like to serve this cake with fresh raspberries and raspberry sauce to balance the richness of the cake.

Ingredients

480g dark or bittersweet chocolate

500g butter

250mL 'espresso' or other very strong coffee

1 cup packed brown sugar

8 large eggs

1kg frozen raspberries, thawed

juice of 1 lemon

2 tablespoons sugar

2 punnets fresh raspberries

Method

1. Preheat the oven to 180°C and butter a 24cm non-stick cake tin or long non-stick loaf tin (not springform).

2. Chop the chocolate and place in a large heatproof bowl.

3. In a small saucepan, bring the butter, espresso and sugar to the boil and simmer briefly. Pour the liquid over the chopped chocolate and allow to sit for a few minutes. Stir the ingredients gently to help the chocolate melt. Beat the eggs, then add to the chocolate mixture, whisking thoroughly.

4. Pour the batter into the prepared cake tin, then place the tin in a large roasting pan or baking dish. Pour in hot (not boiling) water to reach halfway up the sides of the cake tin, then bake for 1 hour. Remove the cake from the water bath and chill overnight.

5. The next day, remove the cake from the tin. If you find this difficult, fill the kitchen sink with about 4cm of boiling water and dip the cake tin base in the water for a few seconds to loosen the cake. Run a knife or spatula around the tin then invert the cake onto a platter.

6. To make the raspberry sauce, purée the thawed berries and their juice with lemon juice and sugar. Pour the sauce through a sieve then chill for up to two days. Although it will not taste sweet, the acidity will be a perfect foil for the cake. Serve the cake with raspberry sauce and fresh raspberries. You may like a little fresh cream on the side.

Pennsylvania Dutch Pumpkin *Cake*

The 'Pennsylvania Dutch' communities in America have a long history of delicious foods made with only natural ingredients. The founders of these communities travelled to the United States from Holland in the early eighteenth century in order to enjoy the religious freedom of the New World. These communities are more often known by the name 'Amish'. This superb recipe was given to me while I was in Philadelphia last year, by an Amish lady selling bread and cakes at the 'Reding Terminal', one of Philadelphia's largest markets.

Ingredients

3 cups of plain flour

1 ½ teaspoons baking powder

1 ½ teaspoons baking soda

2 teaspoons cinnamon

1 teaspoon ground nutmeg

1 teaspoon ground cloves

1 teaspoon ground allspice

250g butter, softened

1 cup sugar

4 large eggs

2 cups of cooked, mashed pumpkin (about 500g)

1 tablespoon fresh minced ginger

1 teaspoon vanilla essence

½ cup currants

icing sugar, for dusting

pure fresh cream, flavoured with ground ginger and vanilla essence, for serving

Method

1. Preheat the oven to 180°C and butter a babka tin (or fluted cake tin) or a long loaf tin (30 x 12cm).

2. In a large bowl, mix together the flour, baking powder, baking soda, cinnamon, nutmeg, cloves and allspice and set aside. In a mixer, cream together the butter and sugar until light and fluffy, then add the eggs, one at a time, and beat well after each addition.

3. Add the mashed pumpkin, minced ginger and vanilla and mix thoroughly. Add the dry flour mixture and currants and continue to mix gently to combine all the ingredients.

4. Pour the batter into the prepared tin and bake for about 45 minutes for a loaf tin or 55 minutes for a fluted cake tin. When fully cooked, the cake should be a little 'springy' when pressed gently in the centre. Allow to cool in the tin, then unmould. Dust the cake with icing sugar.

5. Serve with pure fresh cream that has been flavoured with ground ginger and vanilla essence.

Hawaiian Tropics *Cheesecake*

This delightful cheesecake is full of fresh, tropical flavours. When testing this recipe, I found that a crust detracted from the fresh flavour of the fruit, so I have opted for no crust and the result is a superb but very light dessert. For texture, I like to sprinkle some crushed macadamia nuts on the base of the tin.

Ingredients

200g macadamia nuts, roasted and chopped

500g cream cheese

1 cup of caster sugar

800g fresh ricotta cheese

2 tablespoons flour

2 teaspoons ground ginger

6 large eggs

1 x 440g can of mango slices, drained and puréed

1 large mango, peeled and diced

1/4 red pawpaw, peeled and diced

2 passionfruit

Method

1 Preheat the oven to 210°C and line a 24–26cm non-stick, springform cake tin by removing the sides and placing a large piece of baking paper over the base. Replace the sides, resulting in a tight false paper base. Butter the sides of the tin. Sprinkle the roasted and chopped macadamia nuts over the base and set aside.

2 In an electric mixer, beat the cream cheese and sugar until the mixture is smooth. Add the ricotta, flour and ginger and beat until just combined. Add the eggs, one at a time and beating well after each addition. Add half the mango purée, folding through by hand to achieve a swirling effect.

3 Spoon the batter into the prepared cake tin, taking care not to disturb the placement of the crushed nuts. Sprinkle the diced mango and pawpaw over the surface. Bake the cheesecake at 210°C for 10 minutes then reduce the heat to 160°C. Bake for a further 50 minutes until the cake has set and the centre is still a touch 'wobbly' (you can check for this by gently shaking the tin).

4 Leave the cake to cool in the oven (that has been turned off) overnight or for at least 8 hours. Transfer the cheesecake to the fridge until required. Before serving, remove the cheesecake from the cake tin and discard the baking paper.

5 To serve, mix the remaining mango purée with the passionfruit pulp and spoon a little of this around each slice of cheesecake. Serve with fresh cream if desired.

Variation: Bake the cheese cake without the fruit topping, and serve the fruit, sliced, on the top or side of the cake.

The Cakes of the Asia Pacific

I had an immense amount of fun creating recipes for this chapter. While I had some traditional Australian flavours to draw on, like lemon cheesecake and lumberjack cake, I set about developing recipes for cakes simply based on a theme. For example, Australians are familiar with Anzac biscuits, those deliciously crunchy biscuits, baked by families of soldiers during World War I, to sustain them and also to raise money for them on their return. I took the flavours of Anzac biscuits and created a cake in honour of those tasty morsels.

When I set about creating Asian cake recipes, I had an empty slate. Asians do not have a tradition of cakes, so I borrowed heavily on flavours such as citrus, coconut, nutmeg, ginger, Chinese tea etc., and came up with a whole host of new and delicious recipes for you.

Most of these cakes make fantastic desserts, as well as superb afternoon tea choices.

Modern Anzac *Cake*

Anzac biscuits have been a favourite in Australia and New Zealand for decades. The letters in the biscuit name actually represent 'Australia and New Zealand Army Corps'. These biscuits were baked and sent to our soldiers during the first World War and stayed fresh long enough to reach the soldiers.

I created this cake from the basics of that original recipe – oats, golden syrup and nuts, and added some cocoa to give it a new dimension. This cake is for the child in everyone.

Ingredients

For the Cake:

125g butter, softened

200g sugar

2 eggs

1 teaspoon vanilla essence

85g ground almonds

3 tablespoons cocoa

30g shredded coconut

200g self raising flour

320g sour cream

125mL espresso –
or strong black coffee

For the Topping:

150mL water

1 cup sugar

4 tablespoons golden syrup

80g tablespoons butter

150g flaked almonds

30g shredded coconut

30g rolled oats

Method

1. Preheat the oven to 160°C and grease and line a 24cm (9") cake tin.

2. Cream the butter and sugar together until thick and pale, then add the eggs one at a time, beating well after each addition. Add the vanilla and mix well to combine.

3. In a separate bowl, mix together the almonds, cocoa, coconut and flour.

4. Fold half the flour mixture into the batter with the sour cream and combine gently. Add the remaining flour mixture with the coffee and mix well.

5. Bake in the preheated oven for 1 hour until puffed and cooked through.

6. Meanwhile, place the water and sugar in a small saucepan and heat gently while stirring to dissolve the sugar granules. When the mixture begins to boil, stop stirring and simmer for about 5 minutes, brushing down the sides of the pan with a pastry brush. When the mixture is pale gold, remove from the heat and stir in the golden syrup, butter, almonds, coconut and rolled oats and stir thoroughly, returning to the heat if necessary to help you mix the ingredients well. After the cake has cooked for one hour, remove from the oven and pour this mixture over the cake, then return to the oven for 10 minutes or until the topping has set.

7. Remove the cake from the oven and allow to cool in the tin for 10 minutes. Use a knife to loosen any toffee from the sides of the tin, then remove the cake and cool completely on a wire rack. as a mid meal snack or serve as a superb winter dessert (see introduction to this recipe).

Chinese Ginger Syrup *Cake* (photographed on page 75)

The Chinese are well known for their love of ginger, and it is traditional on festive occasions to give a gift of preserved ginger. This recipe was given to me by a friend, living in Hong Kong, who finally found a way to use the glut of ginger she accumulated every Christmas.

Ingredients

I cup of mild crystallised ginger

I ½ cups of water

½ cup brown sugar

½ cup of honey

½ cup brown sugar, extra

¼ cup white sugar

125g butter, softened

2 large eggs

I ½ cups self raising flour

½ cup of milk

thick pure cream, for serving

Method

1. Preheat the oven to 170°C and butter a 20cm non-stick cake tin.

2. First, prepare the ginger. In a medium saucepan, place the ginger, water, brown sugar and honey, and bring to the boil. Simmer for 10 minutes then cool. Set aside.

3. Using an electric mixer, cream the extra brown sugar, white sugar and butter together until thick and creamy. Remove the bowl from the mixer and add the eggs, one at a time, beating well by hand after each addition.

4. Add the flour and milk and stir gently, but thoroughly. Remove the ginger from the syrup and slice thinly, then add 3⁄4 of the ginger to the cake, stirring to distribute the ginger.

5. Pour the cake batter into the prepared tin and bake at 170°C for one hour, or until the cake appears firm and dry on top and yields gently to pressure when pressed in the centre with your finger.

6. When the cake has been removed from the oven, spoon the ginger syrup over the cake and allow it to soak into the cake, then turn out and cool thoroughly on a wire rack.

7. To serve, spoon some thick, pure cream on top of the cake and decorate with the remaining slices of ginger. Alternatively, serve the cream on the side of the cake, with the ginger slices folded through the cream or on top of the cake.

Lumberjack *Cake*

This moist, 'full of flavour' cake is perfect any time of day. The rich topping imparts a delicious richness that makes the cake quite festive. It keeps beautifully for several days and is lovely served warm with cream or ice-cream.

Ingredients

For the Cake:

2 medium apples

185g dates, stoned and chopped

1 teaspoon bicarbonate of soda

1 cup of boiling water

125g butter

1 cup of sugar

1 egg

1 teaspoon vanilla essence

1 ½ cups self raising flour

For the Topping:

100g butter

½ cup milk

¾ cup brown sugar

150g shredded coconut

Method

1 Preheat the oven to 180°C and butter a 20cm non-stick, springform cake tin.

2 Peel, core and chop the apples, then combine the chopped apples, dates, bicarbonate of soda and boiling water and allow the mixture to cool.

3 Cream the butter and sugar until light, then add the egg and vanilla, beating well. Add the flour to the butter mixture, alternately with the fruit mixture.

4 Pour into a buttered 20cm cake tin and bake at 180°C for 60 minutes.

5 Meanwhile, make the topping. In a saucepan, heat the butter and milk, then add the sugar and coconut and simmer for two minutes until thick.

6 When the cake has finished baking, remove from the oven and pour the topping over. Return the cake to the oven for 15 minutes. If necessary, grill the top of the cake to darken the colour of the topping.

7 Allow the cake to cool in the tin, then serve warm or at room temperature.

Aussie Lemon *Cheesecake*

This recipe has evolved over the years, adopting tastes and flavours from other recipes, until I reached what I think is the perfect lemon cheesecake with the right amount of lemon and a filling that is not too sweet. The crunchy crust makes a lovely contrast in texture.

Ingredients

For the Crust:

1 cup of pistachio nuts

¾ cup of cornflakes

50g caster sugar

100g butter, melted

For the Filling:

500g cream cheese

500g fresh ricotta cheese

4 large eggs

400g can sweetened condensed milk

¼ cup sugar

juice and zest of 3 lemons

icing sugar, for dusting

Method

1 Toast the nuts until golden, either in the microwave on 'high' for a two minutes or in the oven.

2 In a food processor, crush nuts, cornflakes and sugar until coarsely ground. Add the butter and process until the crumbs are moistened. Press this mixture into the base of a buttered and lined 24cm springform cake tin.

3 Chill until required.

4 In a mixer, beat the cream cheese and ricotta together until smooth, then add the eggs, one at a time, beating well after each addition. While beating, add the sweetened milk in a thin stream until it has all been added. Add the sugar and beat until well mixed.

5 Add the juice and zest of the lemons and mix thoroughly until well mixed.

6 Pour the filling into the chilled cake tin and bake at 200°C for 10 minutes, then reduce oven heat to 165°C and continue baking for 40 minutes, or until the centre of the filling is slightly wobbly but the surrounding area is set. Turn off the oven, leaving cake inside. Allow the cake to cool in the oven.

7 When cool, transfer the cake to the fridge until cold.

8 Remove the cake from the tin and serve, dusted with icing sugar.

Note: This recipe also works beautifully without a crust (as photographed). For a 'crustless cheesecake', simply omit the making of the crust and pour the prepared cheese mixture into the lined tin. Start your filling from point (4).

Indonesian Nutmeg *Cake*

The cuisine of Indonesia has been heavily influenced by centuries of traders. The Portuguese, Indians, Arabs and many others have all left their mark on this complex food. This cake is rich and has quite exotic flavours. For a truly decadent treat, serve it with some fresh, clotted cream or pure cream sprinkled with brown sugar.

Ingredients

2 cups of plain flour

2 cups of brown sugar

1 tablespoon mixed spice

2 teaspoons baking powder

130g butter

1 teaspoon bicarbonate of soda

1 egg

2 teaspoons nutmeg

1 cup of milk

2 tablespoons white sugar

Method

1 Preheat the oven to 180°C and generously butter the sides of a 20cm springform cake tin. Remove the sides from the base of the cake tin, then lay a sheet of baking paper over the base. Replace the sides of the cake tin, firmLy locking the paper in place. Set aside.

2 In a large bowl, mix together the flour, brown sugar, mixed spice and baking powder, then rub the butter into the flour mixture until it resembles course breadcrumbs. Spoon almost half of this mixture over the base of the prepared tin.

3 Whisk the bicarbonate of soda, egg and nutmeg into the milk, then add the milk mixture to the remaining flour mixture in the bowl. Stir thoroughly to combine these ingredients.

4 Pour the batter onto the crumbs in the cake tin, then sprinkle the white sugar over the top of the batter.

5 Bake the cake at 180°C for one hour and ten minutes, or until golden brown and 'springy' when pressed gently with your finger in the centre of the cake.

6 Allow to cool in the tin for a few minutes, then turn out and cool thoroughly on a wire rack.

Amanda's Pear Walnut Spice *Cake*

I first met Amanda while I was judging an Apple baking competition in Beechworth, Victoria, during Autumn 1997. What makes Amanda's recipe even more special, is that this 'chef' is only 10 years old. Amanda easily won the children's section of the competition with this stunning cake that is moist, full of lovely flavours and textures and keeps very well. She decided to serve this cake with a caramel sauce which makes an already superb dessert cake even better.

Ingredients

For the Cake:

65mL rum

120g of raisins

2 cups of plain flour

1 ½ teaspoons baking soda

½ teaspoon salt

½ teaspoon nutmeg

1 teaspoon cinnamon

¼ teaspoon mace

¼ teaspoon ground cloves

2 cups caster sugar

1 cup peanut or olive oil

2 teaspoons vanilla essence

2 eggs

2 large Granny Smith apples, peeled, cored and chopped

1 large firm pear, peeled and chopped

100g pecans or walnuts, roughly chopped

For the Caramel Sauce:

150g brown sugar

150mL cream

60g butter

1 teaspoon vanilla essence

Method

1. Preheat the oven to 160°C and generously butter a 25cm springform tin. Line the base with baking paper. Set aside.

2. Heat the rum to warm, then mix the rum and raisins together. Allow to marinate for 30 minutes.

3. In a large bowl, mix together the flour, baking soda, salt, nutmeg, cinnamon, mace and cloves. In a separate bowl, and using an electric mixer, beat together the caster sugar and oil until thick and add the vanilla essence. Add the eggs, one at a time and beating well after each addition.

4. Remove the bowl from the mixer and add the flour mixture, stirring with a wooden spoon. Drain the raisins (discarding the rum) and add to the batter together with the chopped apples, pear and nuts. Stir the mixture briefly to distribute the fruit and nuts, then spoon into the prepared cake tin.

5. Bake at 160°C for 1 ½ hours, until the top of the cake is firm and 'springy' when pressed gently in the centre.

6. Allow the cake to cool in the tin for 30 minutes, then turn out to cool thoroughly.

7. To make the caramel sauce, place all the ingredients in a saucepan and simmer for 3 minutes. Serve the cake drizzled with caramel sauce and a dollop of thick cream if desired.

Coconut Orange Cake *with* Starfruit Glaze

Although this is not an authentic recipe, I created it to serve after a rich Asian meal and found that the flavours of the cake perfectly matched a myriad of Asian flavours. To give this cake an exotic charm, I have finished it with a layer of starfruit and a golden glaze to bring up the flavour and colour of this very pretty fruit. Store in the fridge if keeping overnight.

Ingredients

juice and zest of 3 oranges

250g butter

1/2 cup of sugar

4 large eggs

1 1/2 cups of self raising flour

1/2 teaspoon baking powder

2 teaspoons mixed spice

1 1/2 cups toasted desiccated coconut *see below

1 packed cup of ground almonds

1/2 cup slivered and toasted almonds

70mL dessert wine or Mirin (sweet rice wine)

2/3 cup of orange juice

1 cup sugar

1–2 starfruit, finely sliced

1 tablespoon orange marmalade or apricot jam

fresh cream, for serving

Method

1. Preheat the oven to 180°C and butter a non-stick 22cm cake tin, lining the tin with baking paper. Set aside.

2. Beat the orange zest, butter and sugar together until the mixture is light and fluffy. Add the eggs one at a time and beat all after each addition.

3. In a separate bowl, mix together the flour, baking powder, mixed spice, coconut, ground and slivered almonds.

4. Mix half the flour mixture into the butter mixture with a wooden spoon. Stir in the wine and juice of the oranges then add the remaining flour mixture. Stir gently but thoroughly.

5. Pour the cake batter into the prepared tin and bake at 180°C for 45 minutes. Meanwhile, make the syrup. Simmer together the orange juice and sugar until the sugar has dissolved, then boil for 5 minutes.

6. When the cake has finished baking, pour the syrup carefully over the hot cake and allow the cake to cool in the tin. When the cake has cooked, remove from the tin and decorate with the sliced starfruit. Heat the marmalade and brush over the fruit gently. Serve with a dollop of fresh cream.

* **Note:** Toast the coconut on 'high' in the microwave for about 2 minutes, then mix a little, and cook on "high" additionally, one minute at a time, until the nuts or coconut are as golden as you like.

Lemon Tea and Pear Cake

This dense and delicious cake is similar to a version I enjoyed at a hotel in Kuala Lumpur. The chef explained that the fruit in this cake is soaked in Chinese tea which softens it and makes it fragrant. I have tried several tea versions and have found that my favourite is made when soaking the fruit in lemon tea. Orange Pekoe also works very well. Remember to begin this cake a day before you wish to serve it.

Ingredients

3 cups of boiling water

3 tablespoons honey or sugar

3 tablespoons lemon tea leaves (or Orange Pekoe tea leaves)

100g dried apples, chopped

200g dried pears, chopped

50g raisins

200g butter

200g caster sugar

3 large eggs, separated

150g plain flour

1½ teaspoons baking powder

zest of 1 lemon

100g pine nuts, toasted

icing sugar to serve

thick cream

cinnamon

Method

1 Mix together the boiling water, honey or sugar and tea leaves and infuse for 10 minutes. Strain the liquid, discarding the tea leaves, then add the chopped dried apples, pears and raisins. Allow to soak overnight.

2 The next day, grease a 20cm non-stick cake tin and line with baking paper. Preheat the oven to 165°C.

3 Cream together the butter and 150g of sugar until thick and creamy, adding the egg yolks one at a time and beating well after each addition.

4 Drain the soaked fruit. Mix together the plain flour and baking powder, then add to the creamed mixture with the drained fruit, lemon zest and pine nuts. Mix thoroughly.

5 In a clean bowl, whisk the egg whites until foamy, then add the remaining 50g of sugar and continue beating until stiff peaks form.

6 Gently fold the egg whites into the cake batter, then pour the batter into the prepared tin. Bake at 165°C for one hour and 15 minutes, or until the centre of the cake is firm and 'springy' when depressed. If the depression remains, return the cake to the oven for 10 minutes.

7 Allow the cake to cool thoroughly, then remove from the tin. Dredge in icing sugar and serve with thick cream, mixed with a little cinnamon.

Apple Oatmeal *Cake*

I love homely cakes like this…moist, tender and full of flavour, they remind us of an easier, less stressful life. This is the sort of cake your grandmother might have made.

Ingredients

For the Cake:

1 cup of instant rolled oats

1 1/4 cups boiling water

1/2 cup butter, softened

1/2 cup brown sugar

1/2 cup sugar

2 large eggs

1 teaspoon vanilla essence

1 1/2 cups self raising flour

1 teaspoon cinnamon

1 teaspoon nutmeg

2 green apples, peeled, cored and diced

100g raisins

100g pecan nuts

For the Topping:

1/4 cup butter

1/2 cup evaporated milk

1/2 cup brown sugar

1/2 cup rolled oats

1/2 cup chopped walnuts

1/2 cup chopped pecans

1 cup shredded coconut

Method

1. Preheat the oven to 190°C and butter a 26cm non-stick springform cake tin.

2. Put the rolled oats into a bowl and pour the boiling water over the oats. Allow the oats to soak until all the water has been absorbed.

3. Cream together butter, brown sugar and white sugar until light and fluffy, then add the eggs one at a time and beat well after each addition. Stir the vanilla essence through the mixture.

4. In a separate bowl, mix together the flour, cinnamon and nutmeg. Add half the flour mixture to the batter with the soaked oats, then add the remaining flour mixture.

5. Stir through apples, raisins and pecan nuts and mix just to distribute the ingredients.

6. Pour the batter into the prepared cake tin and bake for 35 minutes. Meanwhile, make the topping. Heat the butter and evaporated milk in a saucepan until simmering, then add the sugar and cook for a further minute. Add the oats, walnuts, pecans and coconut and stir to mix all the ingredients together. Remove the cake from the oven and spoon the topping mix over the cake. Return the cake to the oven for 10 minutes, then grill the topping until deep golden brown, about 2 minutes.

7. Allow the cake to cool thoroughly before removing from the tin. Serve warm or cold.

Vietnamese Mango Cake *with* Nutmeg Cream

The cuisine of Vietnam has been heavily influenced by the French during the colonisation of Vietnam and the Vietnamese therefore have a wonderful baking repertoire. Some of the best French bread can be found in Ho Chi Minh City. This cake marries western technique with Asian ingredients to produce a deliciously different cake.

Ingredients

1 cup of unsalted, roasted macadamia nuts

3 large mangoes, about 750g total weight

250g butter

1 cup of caster sugar

1 teaspoon vanilla essence

4 large eggs

2 cups of plain flour

1 ½ teaspoons baking powder

½ cup of roasted macadamia nuts, chopped

icing sugar

500mL pure cream

1 teaspoon nutmeg

1 mango, sliced, for serving

Method

1. Preheat the oven to 180°C and butter a 22cm non-stick cake tin.

2. Crush the cup of roasted macadamia nuts in a food processor and set aside.

3. Peel the mangoes and dice the flesh, saving as much juice as possible, then reserve some nice pieces of mango (about 80g) and purée the remaining mango flesh with all the reserved juice. You should have about one cup of mango purée.

4. Beat the softened butter and vanilla essence with half the sugar and beat until thick and pale. While beating, add the remaining sugar and beat until all the sugar has been added. Add the eggs, one at a time, and beat well after each addition.

5. In a separate bowl, mix the crushed nuts, flour and baking powder together.

6. Remove the bowl from the mixer and add the flour mixture, stirring well to combine. Add the mango purée and mix gently.

7. Spoon the batter into the prepared tin, then sprinkle the chopped macadamia nuts and reserved diced mango over the batter and swirl through.

8. Bake at 170°C for an hour, then remove the cake from the oven and cool in the tin. When cool, remove the cake from the tin. Dredge with icing sugar.

9. To prepare the cream, sprinkle the nutmeg over, whip the cream and nutmeg together until the cream is thick and fragrant. Serve alongside the cake with some mango slices.

The Cakes of the Subcontinent

When one thinks of the cuisines of India, Pakistan and Sri Lanka, it is rare to think of a baked cake in the style of Western baking.

However, as I researched extensively for this cookbook, I began to find a small but strong tradition of baking – mostly a legacy left over from the influence of the English occupation of the region.

I talked to people with grandparents of English/Indian extraction, associates who were born in India and talked with some who had lived in India for a time but were in the country as visitors only. When I quizzed them about cakes in India, all had a story to tell.

They remembered heavy, coconut and syrup based concoctions that were mixed in a saucepan, then allowed to set in a flat pan – not a 'baked' cake but still very much a cake. Some told me stories of mothers and aunts who baked heavy, flour based sweets that were soaked with spiced sugar syrups, and there were also stories of traditional English style cakes that had been adopted over the years by Indian women who then gave these cakes their own identity by flavouring them with cardamom, ground coriander, cloves and the like.

Many of these recipes have been created and refined by me to make them more suitable for our Western style of baking, but I have stuck, religiously, to the flavours of the Indian kitchen.

Pakistani Spice *Cake*

This rich, golden cake is full of spicy flavours and leaves your mouth with a warm, tingly feeling. It is a perfect accompaniment to a well-made cup of tea, and if you have any left over, makes a wonderful bread and butter pudding. To serve this cake as a dessert, accompany it with some slices of ripe, sweet pineapple.

Ingredients

2 cups of plain flour

1 tablespoon of ginger powder (ground ginger)

2 teaspoons cinnamon

2 teaspoons mixed spice

2 teaspoons baking powder

¾ teaspoon baking soda

1 teaspoon turmeric

¾ cup buttermilk

250g butter, softened

¾ cup caster sugar

2 large eggs

¼ cup molasses

½ cup golden syrup

1 teaspoon vanilla essence

1 cup of fresh, grated coconut

60g crystallised ginger (optional)

Method

1 Preheat the oven to 170°C and generously butter a 24cm non-stick springform cake tin.

2 In a bowl, mix together the flour, ginger, cinnamon, mixed spice, baking powder and baking soda.

3 In a separate small bowl, whisk together the turmeric and buttermilk and set aside.

4 Using an electric mixer, beat together the butter and sugar until thick and fluffy. Beat in the eggs, one at a time and beat well after each addition. With the mixer on the slowest speed, add the molasses, golden syrup, vanilla.

5 Add half the flour mixture and half the buttermilk and fold gently. Add the remaining flour mixture and buttermilk, then fold in the grated coconut and crystallised ginger.

6 Pour the batter into the prepared cake tin and bake at 170°C for 40 minutes, or until the cake is 'springy' when gently pressed in the centre of the cake. Allow the cake to cool for 5 minutes, then turn out onto a wire rack to cool thoroughly.

Variation: Although not at all authentic, this cake is wonderful when crowned with a light, slightly exotic icing. Beat together 200g cream cheese, 100mL thick cream and 100g icing sugar until thick and smooth. Fold through 1 tablespoon minced fresh ginger. Spread over the cooled cake. Serve the iced cake with some fresh mango spears or cut the mango flesh into chunks on the side.

Sri Lankan 'Pastry Cake' (photographed on page 93)

This cake is one of the most popular sweets in Sri Lanka and the recipe was adopted during the Portuguese rule of Sri Lanka. It really is a cross between a cake and a Danish pastry which is why I have given it such an unusual name. In Sri Lanka, it is called 'bolo folhado' which, translated, means 'many layers'.

Ingredients

For the Pastry:

3 cups of plain flour

1 teaspoon cinnamon

200g butter, chilled and diced

1 teaspoon freeze dried yeast

2 tablespoons skim milk powder

1 cup of warm water

1 tablespoon sugar

2 egg yolks and 1 egg for glazing

For the Filling:

3 cups of sugar

2 tablespoons honey

200mL of water

400g raw cashew nuts, finely ground

50g marzipan, chopped

Method

1. Place the flour in a large bowl with the cinnamon and 'rub through' half the butter (100g) until the mixture resembles fine breadcrumbs. Mix the yeast, skim milk powder, sugar and egg yolks with the warm water and whisk well. Make a well in the flour mixture, then pour in the milk mixture and stir using a wooden spoon.

2. When the mixture becomes a 'shaggy mass', turn the dough out onto a floured surface and knead the dough, adding extra flour as necessary if the dough becomes sticky. Continue kneading until the dough is satiny and elastic. Shape the dough into a ball and place it in a clean, oiled bowl. Cover the bowl with a clean kitchen towel or plastic wrap and allow the dough to rise until it has doubled in size, about 2 hours.

3. When the dough has risen, roll it out to a rectangle about 30cm x 60cm. Using a vegetable peeler, shave thin slices of the remaining butter and lay them on the lower two-thirds of the dough, covering the dough until all the butter has been used. Fold the top of the dough down onto the buttered area, then fold the bottom buttered section up. You should now have a neat rectangular block of dough. Using a rolling pin, roll out the dough to a rectangle about 30cm x 60cm, then fold it up again as before. Chill for 30 minutes. Repeat the rolling and folding as above and chill for a further 30 minutes.

4. Meanwhile, make the filling. Mix together the sugar, water and honey and bring to the boil. Simmer together for 5 minutes until thick and syrupy. Remove from the heat and stir in the cashew nuts and chopped marzipan. Return to the heat, just to help the ingredients combine, then remove from the heat and cool completely.

5. Divide the dough into 4 pieces, each one slightly bigger than the last then roll out each to a circle, with the largest piece of dough being rolled out to about 28cm and the others being rolled out to circles a little smaller than the last. (If you stack each circle on the previous one as you roll them out, it will be easy to make sure the sizes are correct.)

6. Beat the remaining egg. Lay the largest circle of dough on an oiled baking tray and spread 1/4 of the filling over the largest circle, leaving 4cm all around the edges. Brush this unfilled area with the beaten egg, then place the next circle of dough over the last. Continue in this way until all the dough and filling have been used up, always remembering to leave a circle of unfilled dough around the edges. Using your fingers, flute or pinch the edges of the pastry decoratively, sealing very well to make sure that the filling doesn't ooze out. Brush the remaining beaten egg over the top of the pastry stack. With the point of a sharp knife, make lots of shallow cuts from the centre of the cake to the edge (like tiny wedges of cake).

7. Bake the cake at 220°C for 10 minutes then turn the heat down to 190°C for a further 30 minutes, or until golden brown and crisp. Cut the cake into thin wedges to serve.

Indian Yoghurt Banana *Cake*

This very dense and rich cake recipe was given to me by a close friend who has spent a great deal of time in India. Although I have modified it slightly, it is still very similar to the version served at the hotel in Bombay where she chooses to stay. It keeps very well and is a perfect ending to a spicy meal.

Ingredients

80g desiccated coconut, toasted

125g ghee or clarified butter (see note)

150g caster sugar

40g brown sugar

2 large eggs

3 medium large bananas, very ripe

200g thick plain yoghurt

250g self raising flour

1 teaspoon cinnamon

½ teaspoon mixed spice

200g sour cream or creme fraîche

100g icing sugar

50g toasted shredded coconut

Method

1 Preheat your oven to 190°C. Remove the base from a 22–24cm non-stick springform tin and place a piece of baking paper (such as 'Glad Bake') over the top. Replace the sides of the tin, causing the paper to form a false base. Grease the tin and pour in the toasted desiccated coconut. Tip the tin all around to coat the greased sides with the coconut, then pour out the excess and reserve for the cake batter.

2 Beat the ghee and sugars in a bowl until creamy, then add the eggs, one at a time, beating well after each addition. Meanwhile, mash the bananas.

3 Remove the bowl from the mixer, then add the mashed bananas, yoghurt, flour, cinnamon, spice and remaining coconut and stir thoroughly with a wooden spoon until all ingredients are well combined and no floury areas remain.

4 Spoon the mixture into the prepared tin and gently smooth the top.

5 Bake at 190°C for 55 minutes, or until firm and 'springy' when depressed in the centre of the cake.

6 Remove from the oven, allow to cool for 15 minutes, then remove the sides of the tin and cool completely.

7 When cool, remove the base and baking paper and place the cake on a platter.

8 To make the icing, mix together the sour cream and icing sugar until thick and spreadable, then spread over the top of the cool cake. Pour the shredded coconut over the cream, until thickly covered.

Note: Ghee is the Indian word for clarified butter which is butter with all the milk solids removed. To make your own ghee, heat double the amount of butter you need, then pour into a glass jug. Allow to cool for 15 minutes, then carefully pour off the clear, golden liquid on top (this is the clarified butter). Discard the milk solids. If you prefer, ghee is available, ready to use, from the dairy case of your supermarket.

Indian Carrot *Cake*

This recipe was inspired by the Indian 'halwa', a type of sweet that is quite crumbly and is served in a similar way to Turkish Delight – with tea or coffee at the end of a meal. This cake is more like the Western style carrot cake, but with the flavours of an Indian kitchen. This cake is fruity, nutty, spicy and pronounced by all my children to be 'fabulous'.

Ingredients

4 large eggs

1 teaspoon ground cardamom (or to taste)

1 teaspoon mixed spice

1/4 teaspoon ground cloves

450g sugar

100g ghee*, softened or vegetable oil

200g carrots, grated

zest of an orange

1/2 cup chopped pistachio nuts, toasted

1/2 cup chopped cashew nuts, toasted

1/2 cup sultanas

230g self raising flour

icing sugar, for serving

Method

1 Preheat the oven to 180°C and butter a large non-stick loaf tin, then dust lightly with flour. Set aside.

2 In a large bowl, mix together the eggs, cardamom, mixed spice, ground cloves, sugar and ghee and whisk until the batter is smooth. Add the carrots, orange zest, nuts and sultanas, then add the flour, mixing thoroughly but gently.

3 Pour the batter into the prepared tin and bake at 180°C for 45 minutes, or until the top of the cake is golden brown and is 'springy' when pressed gently in the centre.

4 Remove the cake from the oven and allow to cool for a few minutes, then turn the cake out of the tin and allow to cool on a wire rack.

5 Dust with icing sugar before serving.

* Ghee is the Indian word for clarified butter, available at supermarkets or Indian grocers, or use the method on page 96 to prepare your own.

Orange Cardamom *Cakes*

This deliciously flavoured batter can be baked into one large cake, but I much prefer to bake it in individual sizes and serve a whole 'baby' cake to each person, complemented by an orange spiked sauce. The idea for this recipe was given to me by a fellow 'foodie' who spent some time in New York, working in various Indian restaurants. I then baked the cakes in small serves and made the orange sauce — perfection! This is the perfect end to a spicy Indian dinner party [serves 10–12].

Ingredients

For the Cakes:

2 cups of plain flour

1½ teaspoons baking powder

1 teaspoon baking soda

2 teaspoons ground cardamom

125mL butter, softened

1 cup sugar

zest and juice of 2 oranges

2 large eggs

⅔ cup yoghurt

2 tablespoons sugar, extra

3 tablespoons marmalade

2 tablespoons boiling water

For the Orange Sauce:

2 cups of sugar

1 cup of water

juice of two oranges

2 tablespoons thick cream

4 large oranges, segmented

Method

1. Preheat the oven to 180°C and generously butter 2 non-stick 'Texas' muffin pans each with 6 cavities.

2. In a large bowl, combine the flour, baking powder, baking soda and ground cardamom. Set aside.

3. Using an electric mixer, cream the butter, sugar and orange zest together until light and fluffy. Add the eggs and yoghurt and mix on low speed until the ingredients are well combined, then fold the flour mixture in by hand – do not over-mix.

4. Divide the batter evenly among the 10–12 muffin cups and bake at 180°C for 15–18 minutes, approximately. Meanwhile, whisk together the fresh orange juice, marmalade, boiling water and extra 2 tablespoons sugar.

5. When the orange cakes are ready to come out of the oven, remove the muffin tins, then spoon the orange syrup over the cakes and allow them to cool in the tins.

6. Meanwhile, make the sauce. Mix together the sugar and water and stir until the sugar has dissolved. Raise the heat and boil vigorously, washing down the sides of the pan with a pastry brush dipped in cold water. Continue boiling until the syrup turns a rich, deep gold then remove the pan from the heat. Carefully add the orange juice to the syrup (be careful because it will splatter). Swirl the pan to dissolve the juice, returning the pan to the heat if necessary. Once the mixture is smooth, remove from the heat and set aside to cool. When cool, whisk in the cream then chill the sauce.

7. To serve, turn out the cakes and place each on a plate, heap the orange segments on top of the cakes, then spoon the sauce all around.

Pistachio Coconut Cake *with* Citrus Syrup

This decadent dessert reminds me very much of 'coconut ice', a pink and white confection from my childhood. This cake is pleasantly green in colour, and this will be intensified depending on the quality of the pistachio nuts you use. The citrus syrup finishes this off perfectly.

Ingredients

3 cups of pistachio kernels, toasted

200g purchased buttercake or 'pound' cake

6 large eggs, separated

2/3 cups sugar

1 teaspoon vanilla essence

zest of an orange

70g coconut threads (or desiccated)

100mL of coconut milk

pinch of cream of tartar

pinch of salt

2 oranges

1 cup of sugar

1/2 cup water

some glacé oranges, to serve

Method

1. Preheat the oven to 180°C and generously butter a 22cm square cake tin.

2. Place the pistachio nuts and buttercake into a food processor and process until finely ground. Transfer this mixture to a large bowl.

3. Using an electric beater, cream the egg yolks, sugar, vanilla and orange zest together until thick and smooth. Fold in the nut mixture by hand, together with the coconut threads and coconut milk.

4. In a separate bowl, beat the egg whites with the cream of tartar and salt until stiff peaks form. Fold a little of the egg whites into the cake batter, then fold the cake batter into the remaining egg white mixture. Mix gently but thoroughly, making sure that the whites have been incorporated. Pour the batter into the prepared tin and bake at 180°C for 30 minutes.

5. Meanwhile, make the syrup. Squeeze as much juice as possible from the oranges and pour the juice into a small saucepan, together with the orange pulp from the juice, sugar and water. Bring to the boil, stirring constantly. When the mixture begins to boil, stop stirring and allow to simmer for 5 minutes. Strain, then cool.

6. When the cake has finished baking, remove it from the oven and allow to cool for 5 minutes. Pour the orange syrup over the cake, then allow the cake to cool thoroughly. When the cake is cold, remove from the cake tin and serve, cut into tiny diamond or square shapes. Cut up the glacé oranges into tiny dice and place a small pile on each piece of cake.

Variation: When baked in a round cake tin, this recipe produces a very rich but lovely dessert cake. Butter a 24cm round cake tin and follow the recipe as above. Serve the cake in small wedges with some pure, thick cream.

Modern Day
Cakes

Modern cakes adopt the style of traditional favourites, and are then updated with sticky caramel sauces, sweet syrups, dense chocolate fillings and more.

Upside down cakes have been popular for a few years and we have a delicious version here for you to try. We also include our favourite, the ever-popular Sticky Macadamia Cake which is our version of sticky date pudding.

Our mud cake is really 'muddy' giving even chocoholics a run for their money!

The poppyseed cheesecake with lemon curd will appeal to cheesecake lovers and will be one you will turn to time and time again.

These cakes will surely be the traditional recipes of the future.

Warm Toffee Macadamia *Cake*

This rich and very satisfying cake will warm the coldest heart. I love to serve it on a chilly winter night when the rain is drumming on the roof and the wind is howling. For a really perfect finale, accompany it with a simple vanilla custard.

Ingredients

100g chopped macadamia nuts

100g chopped brazil nuts

30g shredded coconut

150g brown sugar

80mL cream

60g butter

110g butter, additional

180g white sugar

3 large eggs

1 teaspoon vanilla essence

110mL milk

160g self raising flour

1 teaspoon cinnamon

thick cream or vanilla custard, for serving

Method

1 Preheat the oven to 190°C and generously butter a 20cm non-stick cake tin (do not use springform tins for this recipe), then line the base with baking paper.

2 Mix together the nuts and coconut and toast in the oven, in a dry frypan or in the microwave until golden (see note below). Sprinkle the nut mixture over the base of the prepared tin. Heat the brown sugar, cream and butter in a small saucepan until smooth, then pour over the nut mixture.

3 In a separate bowl, cream the additional butter and white sugar together until light and creamy, then add the eggs, one at a time and beat well after each addition. Add the vanilla and mix well. Fold in the milk, alternately with the flour and cinnamon.

4 Spoon the cake batter over the caramel and spread to the edges of the cake tin, covering the caramel completely.

5 Bake at 190°C for 55 minutes or until the cake is well puffed and firm when gently pressed in the centre. Remove from the oven and carefully turn out onto a cake plate. You may need to spoon a little of the nuts back onto the cake if some stick to the base of the tin.

6 Serve slices warm with thick cream or vanilla custard.

Note: The easiest method of toasting nuts is in the microwave. Place any variety and any quantity of nuts directly on the glass microwave plate, then microwave on 'high' for two minutes. Open the microwave and move the nuts around a little. Continue to cook on 'high' for additional minutes until the nuts are as golden and toasted as you wish them to be. Remember that the nuts will seem soft while they are hot but become very crisp and crunch as they cool down.

Muddy Mud *Cake*

(photographed on page 105)

Mud cakes are increasing in popularity, probably because they keep so well and are incredibly rich and delicious. The true name 'Mississippi Mud Cake' comes from a likeness to the supposedly muddy banks of the Mississippi river. If you would like to make an alcohol free version, simply substitute an equal quantity of juice or milk.

Ingredients

250g butter

250g dark or semi-sweet chocolate, chopped

100g caster sugar

80g brown sugar

20mL brandy

1 ½ cups hot water

185g self raising flour

3 tablespoons Dutch cocoa

2 eggs

1 teaspoon vanilla essence

icing sugar, for dusting

cream or ice cream, for serving

Method

1 Preheat the oven to 150°C and butter a 24cm non-stick, springform cake tin, or small moulds.

2 In a saucepan, melt the butter, then add the chopped chocolate, caster and brown sugars, brandy and hot water. Mix well with a whisk until the mixture is smooth.

3 Mix the flour and cocoa and add to the chocolate mixture with the eggs and vanilla. Beat just until combined. (Do not worry if the mixture is lumpy.)

4 Pour into the prepared cake tin and bake in a preheated oven at 150°C for 50 minutes or the moulds for 30 minutes. Allow to cool in the tin for 15 minutes, then turn out.

5 To serve, dust with icing sugar and serve warm with cream or ice cream.

Variation: I like to cut the cake into individual sized squares and split the square into two. I then fill the cake with vanilla ice cream and pour around hot fudge sauce, which turns this into a hot brownie sundae.

Moulds Variation: Serve with hot fudge sauce.

Whole Orange Syrup *Cake*

This very unusual cake is literally made with whole oranges. It is deliciously fresh and light tasting and keeps well for around 5 days. It can be made the same way with mandarins when they are in season. Just use the equivalent weight of two medium oranges. This cake freezes beautifully for up to six months.

Ingredients

For the Cake:

2 medium oranges

200g butter

1 cup caster sugar

4 eggs

2 cups plain flour

1 cup ground almonds

1/2 cup slivered almonds, toasted

1 teaspoon bicarbonate of soda

1 cup buttermilk

2 teaspoons vanilla essence

For the Syrup:

1 cup sugar

1/2 cup orange juice

2 tablespoons marmalade

clotted cream or rum and raisin ice cream, for serving

Method

1. Preheat the oven to 180°C and butter a 24cm non-stick, springform cake tin.

2. Wash the oranges and place the oranges in a saucepan of water. Bring to the boil and simmer gently for 1 hour. When cool, purée the oranges in a food processor until smooth.

3. Cream the butter and sugar until light and fluffy, then add eggs one at a time, and beating well after each addition. In a separate bowl, mix the flour, ground almonds, slivered almonds and bicarbonate of soda.

4. Add half the flour mixture to the creamed butter mixture, then add half the buttermilk, mix well. Repeat, using all the ingredients, then add the orange purée and vanilla and mix gently.

5. Pour the mixture into the prepared cake tin and bake at 180°C for 60 minutes. The cake is cooked when it is golden brown and bounces back when gently pressed in the centre.

6. Meanwhile, make the syrup. Heat the sugar and juice together stirring all the time to dissolve the sugar. Bring to the boil and cook for 5 minutes. Add the marmalade and stir to dissolve. Spoon or brush the syrup over the cake while still in the tin. Remove the cake from the tin and serve with some clotted cream or rum and raisin ice cream.

Poppyseed *Cheesecake*

This is a superb recipe for a new and interesting cheesecake. Although traditional cheesecakes are baked with a pastry or crumb base, I find that this often detracts from the flavour of the filling. Recently, I made this cake with no base at all, just a lining of poppyseeds, and this was a wonderful alternative. The lemon curd topping can be bought in a jar if you prefer or if you are running short of time.

Ingredients

For the Filling:

1 cup poppyseeds

500g creamed cheese

500g ricotta cheese

1/2 cup of sugar

6 eggs

1 tablespoon vanilla essence

400g can sweetened condensed milk

1 cup lemon curd (see below)

Lemon Curd:

3 lemons, rind grated and juice strained

75g butter

250g sugar

3 large eggs (or 8 yolks, for a richer curd)

Method

1 Preheat the oven to 200°C and generously butter a 24cm non-stick cake tin.

2 Sprinkle about half the poppyseeds over the base and sides of the cake tin, then tip out the excess and reserve with the remaining poppyseeds.

3 Beat the cream cheese and the ricotta in an electric mixer until very smooth, then add the sugar and continue for 2 minutes. Add the eggs, one at a time and beating well after each addition, then finally, add the sweetened milk and vanilla and beat for one more minute. Using a spatula, stir around the sides if necessary. Add the poppyseeds and mix well to distribute them throughout the cheese mixture.

4 Pour the mixture into the prepared tin and smooth the top gently by tapping the tin on the counter. Bake in a preheated oven at 200°C for 10 minutes, then reduce the heat to 160°C and cook for a further 40 minutes, or until the mixture is still slightly 'wobbly'.

5 Allow the cake to cool in the tin, undisturbed until cold. When the cake is cold, carefully smooth the lemon curd over the surface of the cake, then sprinkle the remaining poppyseeds over the entire surface. When the curd is set, remove the side of the tin and serve.

6 This cake can be made up to three days ahead.

Lemon Curd:

1 Place the lemon rind, juice, sugar and butter in the top of a double boiler or in a heatproof bowl over a saucepan of simmering water. Heat, stirring until the sugar dissolves and the mixture is quite warm.

2 Add the eggs and mix very well with a whisk to distribute them thoroughly, and continue stirring while the mixture heats. Keep stirring until the mixture coats the back of a spoon, which indicates that the eggs have thickened and set.

3 Do not allow the mixture to boil because the eggs will curdle. Allow to cool a little, then spread over cake.

Sticky Macadamia Cake with Toffee Sauce

This wonderfully rich cake is my version of sticky date pudding. It has all the moist sweetness of the dates with added crunch from the nuts. The toffee sauce is wonderful warm or cold and keeps well in the fridge for up to one week.

Ingredients

For the Cake:

170g large dates, pitted and chopped

1 teaspoon bicarbonate of soda

300mL boiling water

60g butter

1 cup brown sugar

2 large eggs

170g self raising flour

1 teaspoon vanilla essence

100g macadamia nuts, chopped and toasted

For the Toffee Sauce:

150g brown sugar

150g double cream

1 teaspoon vanilla essence

50g butter

Method

1 Preheat the oven to 180°C and butter an 18cm square tin or individual "dariole" moulds and dust with flour.

2 Mix the dates with the bicarbonate of soda and cover with the boiling water. Cream the butter and sugar until creamy, then add eggs, one at a time. Fold in the flour, date mixture and vanilla essence. Mix well, lastly adding the chopped nuts.

3 Bake at 180°C for 35 minutes (individual moulds 20–25 minutes). The cake should be well puffed and deep brown.

4 Meanwhile mix the brown sugar, cream, vanilla essence and butter in a saucepan. Heat until boiling and simmer for 5 minutes, then cool.

5 To serve, pour the sauce over the warm cake, or, if you prefer, pour the sauce onto individual plates and place the cake on top.

Note: For a really lovely presentation, pour the sauce into a squeeze bottle and zig zag the sauce over the dessert plates, then place the slices of cake on top. Individual moulds make 6.

Banana *and* Raisin Upside Down Toffee Cake

This is the ultimate 'cool weather' dessert cake. Serve it warm or at room temperature with a little clotted cream or creme fraîche for a perfect finish.

Ingredients

For the Topping:

80g butter

200g sugar

100g brown sugar

juice of 1 lemon

2 tablespoons boiling water

For the Cake:

5 firm bananas

1 cup pecan nuts

1 cup raisins

250g butter

250g brown sugar

4 large eggs

250mL buttermilk (or sour cream)

380g self raising flour

1 1/2 teaspoons baking powder

2 teaspoons ground ginger

2 teaspoons cinnamon

1/2 teaspoon ground nutmeg

clotted cream or creme fraîche, for serving

Method

1. Grease a 26cm spring form cake tin and line with a piece of baking paper by placing the paper over the base then replacing and securing the sides of the tin. Set aside.

2. Make the topping first. In a heavy frypan, melt the butter then sprinkle both sugars over the top. Add the juice of the lemon and boiling water, then bring to the boil. Simmer for 10 minutes until the mixture becomes golden brown and caramelised.

3. Slice the bananas into thick, diagonal pieces and add these to the caramel with the nuts and raisins. Cook over a high heat for 3 minutes to coat the ingredients with the caramel, then spoon this mixture into the prepared cake tin. Smooth gently to cover the entire base of the cake tin and set aside.

4. Beat the butter and sugar together until creamy, then add the eggs one at a time, beating well after each addition. Add the buttermilk or sour cream and combine thoroughly by hand. In a separate bowl, combine the flour, baking powder, ginger, cinnamon and nutmeg. Add this to the cake batter and mix thoroughly, but gently, by hand.

5. When the batter is well mixed, pour it over the banana mixture and smooth the top. Bake at 180°C for 75 minutes, or until the surface 'bounces back' when gently pressed in the centre.

6. Allow the cake to stand for 5 minutes, then use a plastic spatula to gently separate the cake from the sides of the tin. Place a flat tray (or platter) over the base of the cake and turn over so that the cake is now the right way up. Remove the sides of the tin, then remove the base of the cake tin and gently peel the paper off, leaving behind the succulent toffee banana topping.

7. Serve warm or at room temperature with clotted cream or creme fraîche.

Savoury *Cakes*

While cakes are not usually associated with savoury ingredients, I have used quite a bit of artistic licence to put together a selection of superb recipes perfect for picnics, buffets and elegant entrées.

I have drawn heavily on the delightful flavours of the Mediterranean with a little bit of Mexico thrown in for good luck.

Pestos, black olives, sun-dried tomatoes, roasted capsicums, fresh herbs and chilli all combine in various ways to produce a delicious selection for you to choose from.

All these recipes can be made ahead of time, in fact most of them require it, leaving you plenty of time to enjoy entertaining your family and friends.

All you'll need to complement these savoury cakes is some crisp white wine and some crusty bread…enjoy!

Savoury Polenta *Cake* (photographed on page 117)

This superb savoury polenta cake comes to us from Beechworth and was created by Karen from the Parlour and Pantry. It is a wonderful choice for entertaining because it needs to be made well ahead of time and reheats very well in the microwave.

Ingredients

9 cups water

1 teaspoon salt

450g instant polenta

100g fresh pesto

100g fresh baby spinach, well washed

2 red capsicums

2 yellow capsicums

1 large eggplant

1 tablespoon olive oil

130g Gruyère cheese, grated

250g tasty cheese, grated

1 1/2 cups of tomato based sauce

Basic Pesto:

2 cups of packed basil leaves

2 cloves garlic

1/2 cup toasted pistachio nuts

1/3 – 1/2 cup olive oil

1/3 cup grated Parmesan cheese

salt and pepper to taste

Pesto Cream (Serving Alternative 1):

1 quantity Basic Pesto

3 cups fresh cream

Roasted Capsicum Sauce (Serving Alternative 2):

4 capsicums, grilled and peeled as per Method

1–2 tablespoons balsamic vinegar

Method

1 Line a 25cm springform tin with plastic wrap and set aside.

2 In a saucepan, bring the water and salt to a rapid boil. Remove the pan from the heat, then add the polenta in a thin stream. Return the pan to the boil and simmer while stirring for 10 minutes until the polenta is thick. Remove the pan from the heat and add the pesto and spinach and stir through to incorporate. Pour into the lined cake tin, smooth the top and allow to cool until firm or overnight.

3 Meanwhile, cut the capsicums into quarters and discard the seeds. Grill the capsicum pieces, skin side up until blistered and beginning to blacken (about 4 minutes). Remove the capsicums from the griller and place them into a plastic bag until cold. When they are cold enough to handle, peel off the skins and discard. Reserve the grilled capsicums for assembling the polenta cake.

4 Slice the eggplant into 5mm rounds and sprinkle with salt. After 30 minutes, wash briefly and dry well. Brush the eggplant pieces with olive oil and grill until golden on each side. Set aside.

5 Mix the grated cheeses together and set aside. When you are ready to assemble the polenta cake, remove the firm polenta from the cake tin. With a sharp knife, slice horizontally into 3 equal layers (like layers of a sponge cake).

6 Line the 25cm cake tin with foil or 'glad bake' and place the bottom layer of polenta on the bottom of the tin. Place half of the roasted capsicum pieces and eggplant slices over the polenta. Top with half of the tomato sauce. Sprinkle one third of the cheese mixture over the tomato sauce. Repeat the above layers of polenta, capsicum, eggplant, tomato sauce and cheese. Place the last layer of polenta over, and sprinkle the remaining cheese over the top.

Savoury Polenta *Cake*

(continued)

7 Bake at 180°C for an hour, then remove from the oven and allow to cool. Leave to set overnight.

8 To serve, reheat in the oven or microwave and drizzle with a basic pesto, pesto cream sauce or roasted capsicum sauce (recipes below).

Basic Pesto:

In a food processor, pack the basil leaves, garlic and nuts and process just until the mixture is chopped. With the motor running, add the oil through the feed tube until the mixture is as thick as you like. Fold in the grated cheese and a little salt and pepper if you like. Store in the fridge in a glass jar, covered with a little extra olive oil, for about 2 months.

Pesto Cream:

Mix equal quantities of pesto and fresh cream and heat together until just warm.

Roasted Capsicum Sauce:

Purée the roasted capsicum pieces with the balsamic vinegar until smooth.

Savoury Eggplant *and* Goats Cheese Cake

Savoury cakes make a surprisingly delightful addition to any meal. They travel well and are just as delicious served warm or cold, making them a perfect choice for a picnic or outdoor dining. This lovely version uses barbecued or char grilled eggplant for extra flavour.

Ingredients

6 medium eggplants (of similar size)

salt

3 cloves garlic, minced

200mL olive oil

2 red capsicums

100g fresh pesto (bought or home-made)

100g rocket (arugula) leaves

200g mild Feta cheese

100g goats cheese

150 grated mozzarella

600mL bottle of your favourite tomato pasta sauce

Method

1 Preheat the oven to 200°C.

2 Wash the eggplants and cut the flesh into even slices about 3/4cm thick. Lay the slices on wire racks and sprinkle with salt. Allow the eggplants to 'de-gorge' for one hour, then wash well. Dry the slices thoroughly.

3 Mix the garlic with the olive oil then brush the slices of eggplant, one side only.

4 Heat a barbecue or grill pan, then cook the eggplant slices (as many as will comfortably fit), oiled side down until golden. Before turning, brush the uncooked side of the eggplant slice, then turn and grill the other side. Remove the cooked slices and place on a wire rack to cool. Continue cooking all the eggplant slices in this way until all are done.

5 Cut the flesh off the capsicums in large pieces and grill these skin side up if using an oven grill, or skin side down if using a grill pan or barbecue. When the skins are blackened, place the capsicum pieces in a plastic bag and allow to cool. Then peel off the skins and cut the capsicum pieces into strips.

6 Lightly oil a deep ceramic pie plate or non-stick cake tin and arrange a layer of eggplant slices over the bottom, overlapping slightly to cover the base. Cover with some rocket leaves, strips of capsicum and dot with pesto, spreading gently. Sprinkle some Feta cheese, goats cheese and mozzarella cheese over the vegetables. Repeat these steps until all ingredients have been used, ending with a layer of eggplant.

7 Bake at 200°C for 30 minutes until hot, then remove from the oven and cool slightly. Serve slices of the eggplant cake with a rich tomato sauce and perhaps a rocket salad.

Individual Basil *and* Sun-dried Tomato Cheesecakes

These lovely little 'cakes' make a superb entrée to an elegant dinner or as a light summer lunch. I like to serve them on a bed of baby lettuce, lightly dressed with olive oil and balsamic vinegar.

Ingredients

2 tablespoons melted butter

1 cup of pistachio kernels, finely chopped

250g cream cheese

250g ricotta cheese

1/2 cup sour cream or yoghurt

2 large eggs

1/2 – 1 teaspoon salt or to taste

2 teaspoons Hungarian mild paprika

1/4 teaspoon freshly ground black pepper

1/2 bunch of chopped chives

12 sun-dried tomatoes in oil, drained

1 cup basil leaves (tightly packed)

sun-dried tomatoes and basil leaves, extra

2 tablespoons sour cream, extra

Method

1 Preheat the oven to 190°C.

2 Generously grease a 'Texas size' muffin tin with six indentations, or alternatively 6 large soufflé dishes. Sprinkle the chopped nuts over the inside of each muffin indentation or soufflé dish so that they are entirely coated.

3 In a large mixing bowl, beat the cream cheese and ricotta cheese together until well mixed, then add the sour cream (or yoghurt), eggs, salt and pepper to taste, and the paprika, and beat well until smooth. Add the chopped chives and set aside.

4 Finely chop the sun-dried tomatoes and slice the basil leaves finely. Add to the cheese mixture and stir thoroughly.

5 Spoon the mixture into the prepared muffin tin or soufflé dishes and bake at 190°C for 15 minutes. Reduce the heat to 140°C and bake for a further 10 minutes. Remove from the oven and set aside to cool.

6 Turn the little cheesecakes out of the tins and serve warm or cold garnished with extra sun-dried tomatoes, basil and sour cream or with a side salad.

Note: To serve warm, it is better to bake the cheesecakes ahead and cool, then reheat gently in the microwave oven.

Mexican Tortilla *Cake*

This fabulous 'cake' makes a pleasant change from savoury quiches and tarts. The tortillas are layered with an interesting filling of capsicums, chillies, dried beans and other nutritious ingredients, gently touched with Mexican flavours to give you an elegant and visually impressive result. Although there are lots of ingredients, the making of this 'cake' is surprisingly easy.

Ingredients

2 tablespoons olive oil

1 teaspoon ground cumin

1/2 teaspoon chilli powder

1 red capsicum, diced

1 yellow capsicum, diced

1 small Spanish onion, finely chopped

3 small, fresh green chillies, minced

600mL prepared tomato based pasta sauce

600g cooked cannellini beans (either vacuum sealed, canned and drained or home-cooked)

1/2 bunch of fresh chives, finely chopped

600g cooked brown lentils (either vacuum sealed, canned and drained or home-cooked)

1/2 cup fresh coriander leaves, roughly chopped

1/2 cup grated Mozzarella cheese

1/2 cup grated Gruyère cheese

1/2 cup grated tasty cheese

1 cup chopped parsley

8 x 20cm flour tortillas

1 cup of plain yoghurt

extra coriander leaves

2 tablespoons sour cream, extra

Method

1. Preheat the oil to 170°C.

2. Heat the olive oil and cumin and chilli powder and sauté for one minute until fragrant. Add the red and yellow diced capsicums, chopped Spanish onion and minced chillies and sauté for 5 minutes until the vegetables have softened.

3. Add the tomato based pasta sauce and simmer for 10 minutes until the mixture has reduced slightly, then divide the mixture evenly between two bowls. Add the cannellini beans and chives to one bowl of sauce and add the lentils and coriander to the remaining bowl of sauce. Mix all the cheeses in a bowl with the parsley and mix well.

4. Line a 20cm springform cake tin with foil, making sure that there is plenty of 'overhang' all around, then lightly grease the foil with butter or oil.

5. Place one tortilla on the base of the foil-lined cake tin and top with 1/4 of the lentil/coriander tomato sauce and a generous sprinkle of the cheese mix. Top with another tortilla and top with 1/4 of the bean/chive tomato sauce and another generous sprinkle of cheese. Continue with the layers in this fashion until all the tortillas, sauces and cheeses have been used, ending with a sprinkle of cheese and gently pressing down to compact the layers.

6. Bring the sides of the foil up and over to seal over the cake and bake for 30 minutes, then open up the foil and leave the cheese exposed, and bake for a further 10 minutes.

7. Allow the 'cake' to cool in the tin, then remove the tin and place on a platter. Serve warm or at room temperature, garnished with yoghurt and coriander sprigs.

Conversion Table

Approximate quantities rounded to usable units

Metric cup measures are available in most countries; it is advisable to use them instead of guessing or using a kitchen cup. The conversion quantities given are approximate, rounded to the most practical unit; they are not as accurate as the metric measurements. My recipes use the Australian tablespoon that is 20g. Beware that American tablespoons measure 15g, so an additional level teaspoon of the ingredient must be used to achieve the same result.

LIQUIDS

1 metric cup = 250mL

½ metric cup = 125mL

⅓ metric cup = 80mL

¼ metric cup = 65mL

DRY INGREDIENTS

50g = approximately 2oz

100g = approximately 4oz

250g = approximately 8½oz

450g = approximately 16 oz

SPOONS

1 teaspoon = 5g

1 tablespoon = 20g

OVEN TEMPERATURE

140°C / 275°F / gas mark 1

160°C / 325°F / gas mark 3

180°C / 350°F / gas mark 4

200°C / 400°F / gas mark 6

240°C / 475°F / gas mark 9

glossary

almond meal: almond flour or ground almonds

biscuits: cookies in the US

capsicum: bell pepper

caster sugar: superfine sugar

chillies: chilli peppers

cocoa: cocoa powder

cooking chocolate: baking chocolate

coriander: cilantro

cornflour: cornstarch

demerara sugar: known as turbinado in the US, partially refined sugar

double cream: whipping cream

entrée: in Australia and Europe, the "entry" or hors d'oeuvre; in the US entrée means the main course

feta: a salty, Greek-style white cheese made from ewes' milk

gelatine: gelatin in the US

halva: halvah

icing sugar: confectioners' sugar

jam: jelly in the US

minced: ground into very small pieces

plain flour: all-purpose flour

raisin: dried plums

pesto: a sauce of basil, garlic, pine nuts and Parmesan cheese blended in olive oil

polenta: a meal made from maize or corn, usually boiled to make a porridge which sets when cooled and is then fried or baked

punnet: small basket about 8 oz

ricotta: a white, soft cheese-like product made from whey; a by-product of the cheesemaking process

sauté: to cook or brown in a small amount of hot fat.

self raising flour: self-rising flour in the US

semolina: a granular wheat flour, used to make pasta

silverbeet: Swiss chard

springform tin: cheesecake pan

sultanas: golden raisins

sun-dried tomatoes: dried tomatoes

tasty cheese: American cheese

thickened cream: whipping cream

Vialone Nano rice: Arborio rice, an Italian, short and plump-grained rice used in risotto

wholemeal flour: whole wheat flour

zest: thin outer layer of citrus fruits containing the aromatic citrus oil. It is usually thinly pared with a vegetable peeler, or grated with a zester or grater to separate it from the bitter white pith underneath.

Index